PORTUGAL AND ITS EMPIRE:
THE TRUTH

PORTUGAL AND ITS EMPIRE:
THE TRUTH

by

ANTONIO DE FIGUEIREDO

LONDON
VICTOR GOLLANCZ LTD
1961

MADE AND PRINTED IN GREAT BRITAIN BY
THE GARDEN CITY PRESS LIMITED
LETCHWORTH, HERTFORDSHIRE

To my little daughter,
Isabel Maria

CONTENTS

"Bury the dead and care for the living"—
the Marquis of Pombal after the Lisbon earthquake, 1755

ACKNOWLEDGMENTS

THE WRITING OF this book was only possible with the help of Miss Elinor Murphy at my publishers, Victor Gollancz Ltd. She delatinized my use of the English language and calmed it down when I got carried away by my theme. I should also like to thank the staff of the British Museum Reading Room for their helpfulness in my research.

Some of the extracts from the speeches of Dr. Salazar are taken from *Portugal*, a Bulletin printed in English and other languages and edited by the Secretariado Nacional de Informacao, others from the *Discursos, etc.* (Antonio de Oliveira Salazar, Coimbra, 1939, *et al*) and the selection that has appeared in English with an introduction by Dr. Salazar himself under the title *Doctrine and Action* (Faber, London, 1939. Translated by R. E. Broughton and Audrey Bell). Translations from Portuguese books are often my own.

INTRODUCTION

On the 23rd January, 1959, I was happily at work at the Lourenço Marques branch of a British bank, where I had been on the staff since 1950, when a colleague told me that the Portuguese State Police were looking for me. As I had often before been held for "investigation", and subsequently released for lack of evidence, I had acquired a rather blasé attitude towards State policemen. In the past I had gone alone to their headquarters in response to phone calls, to avoid embarrassing my managers with the presence of the police in the bank. This time, however, it was to be different, as I realized when I saw two jeep-loads of policemen draw up outside and surround the building. For one wild moment it looked like a hold-up: customers entering and leaving the bank were stopped and questioned, and there was general panic. I alone knew that they had come for me. They had finally and triumphantly caught up with me. As for my colleagues, they came to the verandah to give me an encouraging goodbye, and that is the last I saw of them.

Throughout the modern, white paradise of Lourenço Marques most of my friends were bewildered. Although no news item was published in the censored local Press, the fact that I was well known caused the news to break in a scandal. I myself felt confident that the Police knew little that was concrete about me beyond my general reputation. I was a well-paid employee of an important bank and economic reporter for its commercial intelligence services; I led the usual gay social life, was comparatively well known as a journalist, was married to a Mozambique-born Portuguese, had a daughter, and had just returned from a vacation in Brazil and Europe. Even my wife and my closest friends were unaware of the extent of my political activities and clandestine connections.

Perhaps I should say here, for the benefit of my Anglo-Saxon readers, that if I have been a rebel, if I have made myself the spokesman of a class of down-trodden peasants or allowed a note of indignation to creep into this candid, personal Introduction, I am not a Communist, nor even a Fellow Traveller. My personal rebellion is that of any humane and democratic man in the face of tyranny. As the State Police discovered after ransacking papers at my home, I was the representative of General Delgado's _Movimento Nacional Independente_—an underground organization which began to operate after his unsuccessful candidacy the year before. At twenty-nine I was the youngest member of his board. From the Police perspective I had other sins. I was the author of many pamphlets in underground circulation; lying in my library were manuscripts of books awaiting secret publication; I had connections with foreign periodicals, including _Time_—and, incidentally, had already been several times held by the police because of the occasional news stories that that magazine published on Portuguese politics. My so-called holidays in the Rhodesias, Angola and the Union of South Africa, like my visits to Brazil and Portugal, had all had to do with my political studies or activities. I had connections with such South African liberals as Alan Paton, Senator Rubin and Patrick Duncan. I had been an assistant and friend of Professor Marvin Harris of Columbia University, and Professor James Duffy of Brandeis University, Boston, who had both just published books on Portuguese Africa. I was also involved in the early stages of a conspiracy that cannot even at this late time be revealed without endangering other people. In point of fact, in my solitary confinement, I was quite unsure on what counts I should be accused.

As it turned out, I was once again to be "investigated". During the next three months I became acquainted with some of the methods of the Portuguese State Police, who also attempted to divide the population against me. Their plan was to demoralize me, and over one hundred people were questioned, thirty-seven of whom were arrested. My file also contained private letters and papers of a purely personal nature. I myself knew little of what was happening and was actually questioned very few times. All I could ascertain was that there were two separate processes against me. _Neither of the files could be seen by lawyers, and one of them, marked Processo de Apensacao (Additional Process), was even closed to me, the accused._

Although I was being advised to await developments patiently and to be prepared for any eventuality, I was determined not to be defeated by this sordid regime, whatever the odds. As solitary confinement did not appeal to me, I forced my guards to take me to hospital, by lacerating my chest with a razor blade I had found in a bathroom. For the next two months I was imprisoned in a room there under the twenty-four hour guard of two policemen. The idea the average Portuguese has of the State Police is such that rumours quickly spread that there was a plan to "remove" me, that I was in a coma or already dead. Through the intervention of doctors, I was transferred from the charge of the State Security Police into that of the Public Police, and by one of the paradoxes of dictatorial regimes, most of my new guards were also opposed to the Salazar government. Through some of them I learned that they had been given written orders, signed by a State Police official of most sinister reputation, to have me shot should I be so foolish as to try to get away. To complicate matters further, several of the State Police were masquerading as Security Police and were planning my "escape" with the help of *agents provocateurs* whom I had known before and never suspected.

A commission comprising the best lawyers in town had an audience with the Governor-General of that time, Commander Correia de Barros, and asked that I should be brought to court—but this the Government did not want to permit. The State Police was pressing for my removal from the country. During this time, as I was to learn later, several stories about me were written in the Press in South Africa and New York. The consequent visits of foreign journalists, who were not allowed to see me, deterred the Government from taking any measure which could lead to publicity.

I was summarily banished from Mozambique by a Government order published in the *Official Gazette*. It was an inquisitorial process, culminating with illegalities committed at the highest level. The Governor-General had no legal power to deport me, but only to ban people he deemed inconvenient from living within the territory. I therefore duly applied to be allowed to go to the Union of South Africa before proceeding to Brazil with my wife and six-year-old daughter. Instead, I was driven from hospital at dead of night, in a closed car, and forced to board a plane for Lisbon alone, with no possibility of seeing or speaking to any of my friends. At the airport, a room was specially reserved for me to say farewell to my wife and daughter (who had all along believed that I had had an attack of measles). My wife had reason to be worried: not only were we ruined, but she had been told that I should be re-arrested upon arrival in Lisbon. In the plane ahead of me, the police official had also flown to Lisbon, the Government having given up, in the face of protests, their original plan that he should fly with me in the same plane.

As I took a farewell look at Lourenço Marques from the air, I wondered what my friends could be thinking—whatever they might be told in my name by the State Police, whatever rumours about me might have come to their ears were surely disregarded. This arbitrary act on the part of the State Police was the final and lasting proof that I had neither given up my fight nor relinquished my ideals.

Perhaps it is to the foreign Press reports that I owe the fact that I was not re-arrested upon my arrival in Lisbon. I was merely handed a notice ordering me to call at the Lisbon PIDE (State Police) head-quarters: instead of doing so I went immediately to a hospital. Knowing that I should be watched, I refrained from making any contacts. When I called on the State Police a few days later I managed to see the name of the Inspector in charge of my case written on some papers on a table: he was Mr. Antonio Fernandes Dias. For the time being I heard nothing from him and was able to live without overt police interference, but later I obtained work as an interpreter at the British Trade Fair, and it was there that I noticed a new face heading the Portuguese State Police team with the party accompanying the visiting Princess Margaret. I learned that the new face belonged to Mr. Fernandes Dias. During the evening I managed to approach and speak to him. I told him that I was Antonio de Figueiredo. "I know," he replied. "We must talk one day soon." It was then that I decided to leave for England immediately. With the kind help of Mr. Eric Gorman from Paisley, who had originally employed me as an interpreter for the Fair, I embarked for London, where I arrived on the 23rd June, 1959.

During my imprisonment in Mozambique, I was occasionally visited by friends, all of whom, without exception, asked me the same question: Why did I, a prosperous and happy man, get involved in politics? No one, except my two sisters whom I had meanwhile managed to settle in Mozambique, knew anything of my real background: that if I was an economist it was not through any formal qualification or training, but by my own efforts; that if I had been the Editor of a magazine in Johannesburg it was only after having taught myself English; that I had had no formal education, beyond primary school standard, and that I had started working at ten years old. How could I help being an upholder of the rights of Africans if they appeared to me to be the Mozambique equivalents of the peasants from whom I had myself sprung back home in Portugal?

Political facts and ideas had been fermenting in my mind since I was a boy. Dr. Salazar was already Portugal's strong man when I was born in 1929. I found myself involved in Portuguese politics at the early age of six, when, together with all other primary school children, I had to give the Fascist salute, and, in reply to the questions "Who lives?" and "Who commands?", to repeat in chorus "Portugal, Portugal, Portugal", "Salazar, Salazar, Salazar".

I was a reflective child and this daily routine disturbed me, I used to wonder for hours on end who could possibly be trying to kill Portugal, who this man was whose initial S was marked on the uniforms of "Portuguese Youth" and who made me feel like one of his herd of cattle. Those were times of change. Even members of the teaching staff at our school were being substituted. The kindly principal, Jose Luis, who would give us sweets and show us Scandinavian films, just suddenly disappeared. I could only deduce that this was by command of the omniscient Salazar, and no doubt in my six-year-old mind the seeds of hatred germinated. When I asked my mother what had happened to my friendly headmaster, I was told that he had "gone abroad". Parents could no longer trust their own children for fear that innocent comments on half-remembered scraps of conversation should lead the family into serious trouble. Many years later I was told that Professor Jose had *really* gone abroad: he had been handed over to Franco's men during the Spanish Civil War—and eventually shot.

The fact that I was a robust little boy may have been one of the causes of the early death of my mother. My father died one month after my birth and my mother was left alone to support three children—my two sisters and me. She earned only six pounds a month as a school caretaker and had to stint herself in order to feed us. I always received the lion's share. One of the first things I learnt in life was that the only way to keep warm in winter, when no other form of heating was available, was to lie huddled in bed with the family. I became an expert at avoiding burning cigars and pieces of stone that would hurt my vulnerable feet through the big holes in my shoes. I grew up "poor"—and in my country to be poor is like being a member of a caste.

I often went to the country to see my grandmother. She was an illiterate peasant who had lost count of her age. She had a weather-beaten face with skin as wrinkled and hard as a mask. She was also very poor. Her house was a crude shack built of stones in the hills of Caramulo, fifteen miles from the family residence of Dr. Salazar. We used to carry wood, often stolen on the wayside, for the fire which was our source of heat and light, and on which we cooked. By the fire we would talk. Being so old and illiterate, she was completely out of touch with the modern situation, and I never quite managed to convince her that Dr. Salazar was not a king. "What difference does it make?" she would ask, in her naïve country-woman's way. I have always remembered ruefully one of her unconsciously apt remarks: "If Portugal is so poor a country as they say, then it cannot afford rich men."

At ten, too old for primary school and as my mother was anyhow unable to keep me at school any longer, I was selling shoes in a Lisbon store and supplying fifteen per cent of the family income with my one pound a month. My mother had been ill for a very long time and in 1943 she suddenly died. At her funeral our richer relatives did not care to join the simple procession, as it was on foot, and the cemetery was a long way off on a hill—besides, I was a solitary small boy dressed in ragged clothes and broken shoes. How could they acknowledge such family ties? My sisters and I were given into the indifferent care of an aunt, who had a scrap-iron business at my birthplace, Figueira da Foz. To avoid untidying the one large guest-room in her house, I was made to sleep in a small room attached to the large barn-like building that housed her business. The door of this small room led on to the street and had no lock. The building was old and decrepit and infested with rats and vermin: I would frequently waken in the night to find rats crawling over me.

At seventeen I emigrated alone to Africa to settle in Beira, Mozambique. I went by "Third Class B", because there was no "Third Class C". The boat on which I travelled was appropriately called the *Colonial* and took thirty-seven days to get to Beira. Almost upon arrival I realized that the African was not in good social shape either. Passing an elderly African whom I had seen in my new home, I took my hat off and was promptly reprimanded as a fool who would let the white community down. Here the people of my social level were not called "poor"—they were called "natives". Their condition was not a result of "unfortunate circumstances", they were "savages", and it would take them many centuries before they could even attain the status of "poor".

Somehow I started reading poetry and became a rather absent-minded young man. I soon lost my first job with the Shell Company for dreamily smoking a cigarette while sitting on a massive drum of oil. I became a radio announcer, and subsequently joined the Army and went to Lourenço Marques. One day, as I was looking for a job, I went to a British bank where a kind Manager gave me employment on the strength of my hazy (though he did not know this) knowledge of English. At first I pretended I was a little deaf and benefited from the fact that everybody was very busy. Besides, there would always be a Portuguese colleague who would quickly translate the odd word for me, and gradually my English improved, until, after a few years, I became economic reporter for the Bank magazine.

This book is written therefore by a man who has reason to be a rebel. I was born in a nation that officially founds its principles on the motto *Deus, Patria e Familia*—"God, Country and Family". But as I grew up I began to understand that not only was God forgotten but also the teachings of Christ about the equality of man and the worldliness of wealth, which were conveniently replaced by the image of Our Lady of Fatima, who smiles alike upon the sins of the rich and the needs of the poor. As I ascended in social scale, travelled and accumulated experience, I realized that our "nation" was a mass of poor people ruled by a small minority who made the laws and had the power to implement them. As I read the suppressed or forgotten books of Portuguese history I understood that much official information had been falsified. As I grew up and became more observant, I was gradually aware of the immense moral corruption around me. People were paid to denounce others; the rigid public and literary censorship was enforced by men who had studied philosophy and the humanities; misleading the poor deliberately was an accepted habit. Even popular sayings which have been repeated for generations without thought revealed to me the facts of an enduring social injustice. In Portugal, when a man is poor he is often described as *um individuo que nao tem onde cair morto*—"someone who has no place in which to fall dead". In spite of social inequalities Portuguese people are taught from Primary school that it is patriotic to hide their misery from foreigners. *Para Ingles ver*—"for English to see" is a popular phrase that is used in connection with the need to "keep up appearances". It not only reveals the impact of the centuries-old ties with England, but the extent to which the ruling class has managed to make the people believe that keeping up appearances for them is a matter of duty. As for the family, feelings, except of course the love of parents for their children, often fail to resist fortuitous changes in a person's social status. One finds people who are ashamed of their own parents, their brothers, their sisters and cousins. Family as the social nucleus *par excellence*, which, according to Dr. Salazar, is one of the key principles of the regime, takes on an ugly appearance of a device to justify the transmission of wealth and the maintenance of the ruling caste.

In Lourenço Marques my social contacts ranged from some of the most senior white Government officials to the humblest African office cleaner. I often went to the country by myself and listened for hours on end to Africans as I had listened to Portuguese peasants. Trying to see the world through their eyes I could understand the fallacy of the professorial theories constructed on their behalf. Speaking of assimilation, they would ask: "How would you like to become an Englishman?" On the subject of race relations, they would point out the existing social inequalities between white and black; they would describe their own inarticulate confusion as the product of subjection. "We are like chicken: we live and move in the same chicken run, but we hardly communicate with each other." I am sorry that I, an agnostic from a country of Catholics should be the one to call attention to this example of man's inhumanity to man—and to be exiled for doing so.

I felt that I should do something for these people, and I began to study law and to apply my knowledge of economics to writing. I also helped visiting Professors with material for their books. One of those whom I helped was Professor Harris, of Columbia University, who stayed in Mozambique for almost a year. To him I owe my improved English and a certain guidance in my studies in sociology.

Even the circumstances of my arrest (I was denounced by Africans and kept under guard by white peasants in police uniforms) proved to me that the combination of ignorance and mystification fashions a virtually impregnable citadel. When a policeman guarding me exclaimed with scorn, "Why you, who had a family and a car and earned more than one hundred and twenty pounds a month, had to do this, I do not know!" I sadly replied that, amongst other reasons, it was *because* I earned more than the combined incomes of the six African office boys ('boys' who were all between forty and sixty) who had, between them, to feed over twenty-five people; or, if he chose, because my salary was more than three times the amount an ordinary white policeman would get to keep a watch on me. When he looked at me, puzzled, I could not help but reflect that in the modern Portuguese world it is impossible to be humanitarian without appearing to be mad.

The aim of this book is to provide foreign public opinion with a comprehensive survey of the problems confronting Portugal and its Empire. It is not only my own first published book, it is the first book on contemporary Portuguese politics ever written in any language by a Portuguese born and educated under the Salazar regime. Since the Portuguese cannot discuss the subject, and foreign students find it hard to penetrate the barriers of language and censorship, there is hardly any bibliography available on some of the subjects covered. Its publication would be impossible in Portugal, where its circulation would endanger those who dared to distribute it as much as myself. The fact that I should risk between eight and sixteen years in jail is in itself an indication of the conditions that prevail.

In writing the book I have borne in mind that it is hardly possible to understand the complex phenomenology of Portuguese colonial policies except in the context of Metropolitan Portugal and its official culture. I have therefore devoted the first half of my book to an interpretation of the Portuguese contemporary scene. I have sketched the personality of its central figure, Dr. Salazar, and made a comparative analysis between his regime and those of the defunct Nazi and Fascist systems. After exposing the dramatic contrasts in social conditions within Portugal, I have also tried to show how little the historic wealth and glory of the Empire has served to enrich the nation as a whole. The second half of the book deals with the Empire, or rather those territories of the economic Empire than have any real political significance. In order to analyse the main themes of Portuguese colonial policies as clearly as possible, I have first examined forced labour and its importance in the social and economic structure of Portuguese Africa as a whole, and then chosen Mozambique as the testing-ground of the "assimilation" system. It should be made clear, however, that my criticism of the policy that uses economic expansion based on African labour to increase white immigration, rather than to hasten the integration and social development of Africans, could apply equally to Angola (as indeed to most white-dominated countries in Africa). In the same way, for the sake of concentration, I have selected Angola as the field for my study of racial problems and the rise of African nationalism. My concluding chapter is necessarily an expression of individual views, but I believe that, in whole or in part, they form the background of most democratic thought in Portugal.

I must ask the indulgence of Engish readers, who should understand that I have written in what is for me a foreign language, while Portuguese intellectuals should realize that this study, being merely a selection of facts that I have felt to be of basic importance to world public opinion, is not intended to be exhaustive on the subject of Portuguese politics. I am well aware that I have not mentioned the names of every Portuguese protagonist of the opposition cause or covered every event of our democratic struggle: to have done so would have involved lengthy explanations for the benefit of foreign readers.

I am quite sure that this book will be found very controversial in my own country, but I only hope that the ethics of the Portuguese nationalist Press will allow it to be respected as the expression of ideas that I as a Portuguese have a right to hold. I hope, too, that those Portuguese who will no doubt read and circulate this book at the risk of imprisonment will understand why I have chosen this moment to express my rebellion against our "nation" and the culture imposed on it. In the first place, I, who am so Portuguese that three of my grandparents were illiterate, am tired of hearing our people dismissed by the world either as "slavers" or ignorant and prejudiced peasants. Secondly, I believe that I should speak in a universal language that I happen to have learned on behalf of the many who are silenced, even in their own tongue. I can assure my compatriots that I am not trying to sell the Empire in Covent Garden, that I have consistently refused to support violent revolutionary movements in Africa, and that I have no connections with either Wall Street or the Kremlin. Nothing would have been easier, for that matter, than to have sold myself to the Estado Novo in exchange for the comforts of my social position in Mozambique, for I have recently been granted permission to return there by a generous change of heart on the part of the Government.

I wrote this book for the same reasons that I fought for the rights and values of ordinary Portuguese and Africans in the years before violence broke out in the Empire: because I share as a human being their thirst for justice and freedom.

A. F.

London, 30th May, 1961

Chapter I

SALAZAR RISES TO POWER

The Illiterates and the Noblemen

At the beginning of this century over sixty per cent of Portuguese adults were illiterate. Together with those who had only rudimentary education and whose reading hardly went beyond the Roman Catholic catechism, they formed the bulk of what was known as the Kingdom of Portugal. They had never heard of a Magna Carta, and their hard daily routine as peasants and fishermen had not changed in centuries.

They had an idea of an immense Empire overseas, somewhere in remote Africa and India, for it had been from amongst the numbers of their ancestors and relatives that the Kingdom had picked the craftsmen who built the armadas of the navigators and recruited the sailors and soldiers for its successive wars of conquest, occupation and repression. But the nearest they had got to the gold and riches of this fabulous Empire had been in the capacity of domestic servants and stable-keepers in the houses of retired and visiting overseas lords.

For this mass of people the battles over a Constitution which took place in the middle of the nineteenth century had appeared to be largely the concern of the noble and powerful. The process of liberal struggle had started in Brazil decades before, when Portuguese sided with Brazilian liberals on the issues of slavery and Independence (achieved in 1822). But the extension of this campaign to Europe, when the liberated Brazilians tried to help in the awakening of the still feudal Portuguese peasants was slowly curbed and they had fallen back into the sleep of centuries. In 1870, when the Kingdom's first Ministry of Education had just been created, they had been quite unable to understand the implications of the Lisbon lectures of a group of leading thinkers who, against all traditional belief, dared to proclaim that Catholicism in Portugal was a force of obscurantism and of intolerance, and a departure from the genuine principles of Christianity itself. Peasants in the mass were much too busy trying to earn a bare

subsistence from their own diminutive holdings, or in the employment of large family estates. Whatever rumours of these novel ideas
reached them met in their simple minds with the superstitious fear of
a God of Terror—for they had been taught, and their parents before
them, that the mysterious force of God was everywhere, knew everything, and often punished new doubts and challenges to the Holy
Mother Church by making their children ill and causing the failure of
their crops.

For these people, the possibility of emigrating to distant Brazil, and
perhaps returning one day rich enough to buy the best house and the
best land in the neighbourhood, and to make friends with the local
priest and other wealthy retired *brasileiros*, was the only achievement
that was really worth hoping for. The ideals of the French Revolution
and the Rights of Man were but the subject of incomprehensible
disputation between the Lisbon and Oporto *senhores*: they sounded
too good to be true. The political struggles in Portugal against the
forces of convention were therefore to be confined to the minority of
urban Portuguese, the discontented middle classes and whatever
workers there were in the incipient industries of the time. Lisbon,
Oporto and Coimbra, and a number of country towns remained the
centres of progressive and liberal agitation.

The excelentissimos senhores and the Republic

The seizure upon Republican ideals as a means of shaking the established values of Portuguese society had started in the second half of
the nineteenth century. The core of Republican intellectuals had
formed themselves into a Republican Party in 1876, and had slowly
managed to gain some popular support, but the proclamation of the
Republic, which followed the assassination of King Carlos I and the
Crown Prince, Luiz Filipe, in 1908, and the deposition of the hurriedly
crowned successor, Manuel II, in 1910, was largely the work of a
handful of anarchists, freemasons, free-thinkers and other idealists,
some of whom had conspired as members of a secret political association—the Carbonaria.

There were revolutionary events at Rotunda, in Lisbon, and other
incidents of political significance, such as the activities of the Coimbra
students, who tore the robes of their Theology professors and slashed
the portraits of former Kings in the sacred Hall of Doctors at the
University, riddling them with bullets. All this served to emphasize not

only the hardening anti-traditionalist mood, but the educated nature of the small-scale, urban conflict. However, whereas the idealists had been able to achieve a certain degree of unity while they had been engaged in struggling for the establishment of the Republic, as soon as the main issue was resolved, and while they were still trying to implement the Republican Constitution of 1911, they soon divided and sub-divided into parties and factions. There were the Evolutionists, lead by Antonio Jose de Almeida, an eloquent, albeit romantic, idealist; the Unionists, headed by good-humoured, irreverent and cynically anti-clerical Brito Camacho; and the Democrats, whose leader was Afonso Costa, a brilliant intellectual.

The First World War came when the Republicans were still keeping an eye on the Monarchists, now disbanded into jail or into exile. The economic and financial conditions they had inherited from the preceding governments were such that, unable to afford the expense of sending an expeditionary force of 25,000 men to the French front, they had to negotiate a financial aid agreement with the Allies. The consequences of Portugal's involvement in the war, both in Europe and in the distant African colonies, were materially disastrous, and the only compensation was the intangible harvest of glory reaped at the Battle of Lys. The repercussions of the war, which obviously extended far beyond 1918, added to the country's heavy and assorted burden of domestic, political and social problems. For a number of years, and in spite of isolated efforts to put things right, the situation threatened to revert to that of the not-so-distant last decades of the Monarchy. Then, in the 1890's, the economy had been on the brink of total collapse, and the bitter joke had been that the only possible way to balance the national budget was to eliminate expenditure.

The landlords, the business men, the underpaid and slowly paid civilian public servants and army officers had reason to be worried. Towards 1920, the budgetary deficits, when converted into gold at the current rate of exchange of each fiscal year, were accumulating at an annual rate of five million pounds, which meant that, within a few years, the deficitary accumulation would be greater than the entire budget. An aggravating factor was the decreasing rate of money remittances from Portuguese emigrants in Brazil, which had traditionally been one of the main sources of relief in filling the chronic gap between imports and exports. Brazil was now having its own share of problems, and, not without some justification, partly blaming the

Portuguese for them. Republican governments in Portugal had to contend with interest rates of eleven per cent on Treasury Bills, while twenty per cent and twenty-five per cent rates for private advances were current throughout the country. The escudo devaluated with imperturbable regularity, from 4s. in 1918 to 2s. in 1922.

Politically, the country, as might be expected, was plunged into anarchy. There was an average of three governments a year, each trying to tackle the situation. In a short time the hundreds of former ministers, acting ministers, would-be ministers and other assorted statesmen were near to becoming yet another social minority. Successive strikes, street fighting, bomb-throwing, political assassination, revolts and conspiracies on the model of the socially and culturally related South American republics, not only made Portugal appear one of the least "respectable" countries of Europe at the time, but rendered the business of administering public affairs, or even thinking of introducing any effective and far-reaching revolutionary measures in the economic and social fields, utterly impossible. The Monarchists and Traditionalists, who formed the hard core of the Portuguese equivalent of a right wing, and whom the Republicans had found divided, had meanwhile, in the frustration of their defeat and in the emotion of their grievances, achieved a working basis of unity. There are historic reasons to believe that, deep down, they were not only enjoying the situation at large, but helping with a peculiar patriotic zeal to complicate matters even further for the Republic.

Armed incursions of Royalists from exile had started right at the beginning of the Republican period. Other manifestations of an embryonic, all-out, anti-progressivist conspiracy are to be found in the unsuccessful movements of Pimenta de Castro in 1915 and Sidonio Pais in 1917. What is more, there was the opposition of the Church, for not only had the Republicans invaded by various ways and means their spiritual domain, but they had dared to think that they could get away easily with the confiscation of Church property.

Traditionally, the Catholic Church had been one of the mainstays of the Monarchy, and the anti-religious character of the Republican regime had been promptly revealed by a series of Bills aiming at the curtailment of the political power of the Church. On 8th October, 1910, three days after the Proclamation of the Republic, a decree had been promulgated to effect laws against the Jesuits and the remaining religious orders. On the 18th the religious oath was abolished; on the

22nd, Catholic teaching in schools was prohibited; on the 23rd the Faculty of Theology in the University of Coimbra closed down; on the 26th Holy Days had become working days; on 3rd November divorce was established in Portugal, and soon afterwards the marriage ceremony became a civil function. Furthermore, in 1920, the Republicans had published the Law of Separation of Church and State, whereby Catholicism ceased to be the established religion of the land, and all ecclesiastical property, from cathedrals to seminaries, had been claimed by the State.

There had always been strong anti-clerical feeling among those who had resented the identification of the Church with the Monarchy and the favours that priests had obtained from kings. This public feeling had taken drastic forms when the Republic was declared, and nuns had been forced to walk round Lisbon with pillows under their skirts to suggest that they had found ways of becoming pregnant inside their convents.

In a country still in the first stages of modern industrialism, and therefore without an explosive labour force, the Progressives were only a section—and incidentally the least rich and powerful section—of the rather intellectual minority of Republican politicians, and there was an immense void between them and the quiet, hard-working and orderly mass of illiterates. Disillusioned, many Liberals began to desert, and became resigned to the notion that, since the Progressives were unable simultaneously to govern the country and to cope with the latent pressures of reaction, perhaps a strong moderate government, which would meet with reactionary approval, would at least achieve some long overdue public order and constructive administrative results.

Meanwhile, the mass of uneducated people went on with their traditional agricultural routine almost indifferent to the complex issues being debated by the minority of urban *senhores*. Protected by their own poverty and backwardness, which has often been euphemistically defined as "rational economy", they hardly felt the material consequences of the national crisis. Not before time, the replacement of a king and his noblemen by a president and his cabinet of civilian *doutores* did much to alter their conception of hereditary rights and the equality of men, but that was about all. Intuitively they realized that, since they had no power or say in their own country, their only hope still remained in emigration to Brazil—the Eldorado of many a would-be rebel of the Portuguese peasant class. All in all, the Republic was a failure. As for any significant revolution in the country's social structure in the short-lived, unfortunate and troubled period of its misrule, a disillusioned Portuguese interpreter aptly summed up the situation in André Maurois' *General Bramble* in these characteristically ironic words: "Now we are all called *excelentissimos senhores*".

Salazar in the Making

After a number of military *pronunciamentos* and forty governments, some well intentioned army officers concluded that "the country was sick". A bloodless *pronunciamento*, headed by Marshal Gomes da Costa, managed to seize power on 28th May, 1926. Parliament was summarily dismissed and a three-man junta was self-appointed. The habit of division was such, however, that the triumvirate did not work out either, and soon only the simple-minded, moderate General Carmona survived. Having succeeded in coping with the uprisings in Oporto and Lisbon in the following year, Carmona set about to look for a new, uncompromised core of collaborators, who could relieve him of the responsibility and burden of his accumulated provisory capacities as both Prime Minister and President.

In 1928 the country's economic situation was further dramatized by a Government appeal to the League of Nations for a substantial loan, which was met with a demand for some measure of international control as a guarantee of repayment. The *excelentissimos senhores* were ripe for surrender, but it was at this stage that Professor of Economics, Doutor António de Oliveira Salazar appeared on the scene.

The son of simple, Catholic peasants who had some smallholdings in the healthy and picturesque region of Santa Comba Dao, Salazar had been a promising student since his earliest years at school. By way of the Catholic Seminary of Viseu, where he later received his secondary education, his modest parents found an economic means of educating the intelligent and well behaved boy above the primary school standards that are the highest education peasant boys can usually afford. While political agitation, both vocal and armed, had been going on in Portugal, Salazar, according to his own official biographers, "grew up in the shade and studied in solitude".[1] In his own words, "he lived absorbed with his ideas and work and was, in short, a boy with a serious idea".[2]

[1] Luiz Teixeira, *Profile of Salazar*, SPN, Lisbon, 1939, p. 13.   [2] *Ibid.*, p. 17.

When he later moved to the more learned shades of the University of Coimbra, he soon became a prominent member of a core of young Catholic intellectuals and a friend of residual Monarchists. He promptly joined the CADC (The Academic Centre of Christian Democrats), whose slogan was "Faith, Study and Action". The centre was then harbouring the young Catholic intellectuals amongst whom there was great enthusiasm over the study of the encyclical social works, Leo XIII's *Rerum Novarum* and *Quadragesimo Anno* by Pius XI. Their place of meeting went under the ominous name of the *Sala do Assalto a Portugal* (Hall of the Assault on Portugal)! Salazar himself had already been the author of a social study, *The Peace of Christ in the Working Class*, and of many articles in the Catholic Press, before he went on his only major visit abroad, to Liège, to attend the Catholic Congress of Working Youth. One of his fellow travellers and best friends, young Dr. Manuel Cerejeira, who was later to become the Cardinal of Lisbon, and who has always had a better sense of humour than the Jesuit layman, Salazar, would later confide that, while he himself had taken the opportunity to have a look round Paris on the way, the serious, black-and-grey-minded Salazar had hardly been out of the headquarters of the various Paris Catholic Associations.

With such virtues, Dr. Salazar had already caught the eye of the *excelentissimos senhores*. As insular as most of those who then held power, Dr. Salazar shared their nationalistic frame of mind. Portugal, as we have seen, was at the time undergoing a particularly depressing national, moral and material crisis. Widely accused of having an incompetent domestic and colonial administration, ridiculed in Brazil and some European countries for the prejudice of its people and the illiteracy of its peasants, the country was financially bankrupt and faced the prospect of losing its African possessions to the dominant imperialist powers. The Portuguese nationalism, which was developing into a mystique at the time, represented an inverted expression of inferiority complexes deeply concealed.

When Dr. Salazar—who has preserved his cultural "purity" to this day by hardly ever travelling abroad—was already an earnest student of economics, at the University of Coimbra, he was still writing in the sincere, schoolboy style of the following passage from a Catholic address:[1] "It is needful for the Portuguese of today to create in the glorious Portugal of tomorrow a strong Portugal, an educated Portugal,

[1] Teixeira, *op. cit.*, p. 19.

a moral Portugal, a hard-working and progressive Portugal. Is it necessary for this purpose that we should love our country deeply? Oh! it is always necessary to love one's own country, just as we love our mother deeply, so let us love our country, the great mother of us all."

The trouble was not so much in his words but in the conception he had of them. The mass of Portuguese people could hardly be more hard working than they were. Since they had had no say in the country's affairs, the educational backwardness of Portugal, its moral and material decadence, could only be blamed on those professors and other men of intellectual and political responsibility who had been selling their brains to wrong and unreal values and issues. It was not for lack of patriotic feeling, either, that the country had been led into its chaotic situation. The trouble lay elsewhere: those Portuguese who were, and are, most susceptible to silly nationalistic inferiority complexes, most ashamed of Portugal's poverty and social conditions, are precisely the rich and the powerful.

However, platitudes such as those expressed in the passage quoted above were bound to find a prompt reception among the men who were then in power, and who, in the circumstances, were displaying a well intentioned, albeit conventional and insular, determination to achieve some measure of national prestige. Tentatively, Dr. Salazar was putting forward in the Catholic daily, Novidades, some of his reflections: "I have long been of the opinion that our social order must undergo certain reforms which time has rendered inevitable, and which, preferably, the right wing itself should conduct, lest the left be called upon to do so, because violence may endanger sacred principles which, for the good of all, should not be tampered with."[1] He added, on an ironic note: "But we need not worry, for everything in this country usually turns out for the best." To his admirers and would-be followers he was already giving some advanced advice. According to a report in the same newspaper shortly before Dr. Salazar took office, he made a speech at the Catholic Centre in which he expounded the policy of the Church, its aims and foundations. "Ordinary Catholics can collaborate with that policy," he stated, and went on to say that Benedict XV recommended the Portuguese Catholics to obey those in authority over them (no matter what the

[1] Novidades, Lisbon, 12.4.28.

form of government or civil constitution of the country), and without reserve, in the furtherance of the common good.

He had not been wasting his time in the shade and solitude. "It is ideas," he said, in *A Minha Resposta*, "that govern and direct the destinies of peoples, and it is great men who have great ideas. And we [Portuguese] have no [great] men"—Salazar's ardent but obscure patriotic feelings seem to have been confined to the inanimate things of Portugal.

This assessment of the situation may have been perfectly correct as far as his own right wing was concerned, but it was an over-simplification, to say the least, if applied to the Left. It is true enough, however, that whenever one of the underprivileged mass of Portuguese people proved to be gifted he tended to emigrate, or managed to climb into another social group, which often made him prejudiced and ashamed of his own origins. The few exceptions, the non-conformists and radicals who remained actively interested in the problems of their own class, had been treated summarily and brutally in Portugal ever since the time of the Inquisition, as, under the control of those who carried on that traditional spirit and often reverted to its methods, organized persecution developed and took new forms.

But perhaps Dr. Salazar's conclusion that Portugal had no great men, whatever this may mean, underlined, rather, the hidden, opportunist ambitions of the dictator-to-be. The simple-minded men in power were watching the respected Professor of Economics: economics was quite an intimidating subject to them, and such a specialist seemed to be the man most needed in the circumstances. Besides, he was not without his friends. The Press at Oporto was hailing him as "a great intelligence, one of the most powerful in the new generation". It was not surprising therefore that Dr. Salazar, indeed a clever man, who appeared as the epitome of all the apparent virtues of the established Portuguese culture, should have been invited to become a dictator. And he was to see to it that the credulous and the parochial should remain to this day his most faithful admirers, even if he had to silence and jail those who could reveal him as an impostor.

Salazar the Saviour

Dr. Salazar's gradual usurpation of power began on the 27th April, 1928, when, on assuming office as Minister of Finance, he publicly announced his "conditions for the acceptance of the Finance Ministry".

Under four points, he essentially imposed on all government departments the obligation to organize their services within the limits of the
financial estimates allotted to them by the budget. In short, the Finance
Minister was to have the right to veto any new legislation involving
increases of current and ordinary expenditure, as well as expenditure
for development purposes. This naïve principle almost looked as if the
Professor of Economics from Coimbra had decided to take seriously
that joke about balancing the national budget by eliminating expenditure. His reasons, however, were far more complex: he was determined to find budgetary solutions, rather than effective economic and
social ones, in order to please and appease those amongst the *excelentissimos senhores* who had most to lose in the event of a more radical
policy.

Since Dr. Salazar, to the best of public knowledge, was not getting
money from heaven, and there were no immediate major increases
in taxation, the process of bringing the budget from a deficit of some
£3 million in 1927-8 to a surplus of £16,000 in the following fiscal
year (the first complete year of his office) could be regarded as the work
of a talented budget director, heartless to the demands of the public
services. Yet, describing the accomplishment of what he himself
defined as the "Dictatorship of Reason and Intelligence", he told a
rather insular audience of heads of Municipal Councils, who had come
to greet him on the 21st October, 1929: "The balancing of our
budget . . . and this idea that the State must always be, shall we say,
'very respectable', form the basis of Portugal's financial reorganization
. . . We performed a feat similar to that accomplished by England,
Austria, Hungary, Czechoslovakia, Germany, Italy, Belgium, France
and all countries that uprose from the ruin of the Great War." This
specific statement shows how keen Dr. Salazar was to have his achievements admired: so keen, in fact, that in the process of trying to provide
his audience with an impressive list of foreign countries for comparison
he simultaneously managed to contradict his self-congratulation.
It seems that, after all, he had only equalled the achievement of practically every Finance Minister in Europe (most of whom, without Dr.
Salazar's special powers, had had to deal with the problems of having
been the very theatre of the war).

When, later, in spite of Portugal's increasing needs, Dr. Salazar's
savings reached higher proportions (and on his departure from the
Finance Ministry the total sum of savings was twenty million pounds),

some modern economists were to think that, instead of being praised, the Finance Minister ought to have been arrested. But by then this was already impossible. Still working in the "shade and solitude", he had seen to it that his budgetary talents were used to buy himself political power with public funds. He was paying reasonably well and promptly the senior army officers and civilian government officials, assuring them a greater security than they had enjoyed before, and, as we shall see, he had been able to underwrite the organization of a huge and expensive repressive machine. Moreover, he was allocating public funds to propaganda on behalf of himself and the regime, at home and abroad, under a specially created Propaganda Secretariat (*Secretariado Nacional de Informacao*), which has done its best to keep the informative ethics of the late Dr. Goebbels alive, while, with sums intended for educational purposes, he was able to finance the Portuguese Youth Movement (*Mocidade Portuguesa*), modelled on the Hitler Youth. One can only conclude, therefore, that he really meant something in his first ministerial speech when he used a phrase to the effect that he knew very well what he wanted and where he was going.

Salazar, the Philosopher Dictator

A bachelor, lonely and determined man, Salazar has often magnetized his visiting admirers from various parts of the country and the overseas territories "with his eyes, his manner and his knowledge of local problems", as a Mozambique settler once confided. He has been described as "addressing the public as if he were talking aloud, alone and to himself".

The nature of his self-imposed dictatorial mission is essentially based on his religious, social and nationalistic beliefs. According to his own admission, one must not "aspire to power as a right, but accept it as a duty, considering the state as God's Ministry for the common good".[1] Far from being perturbed by the opposition of the overwhelming majority of Portuguese intellectuals, and of the ordinary people who not only fail to understand the rhetorical workings of his mind but have given up hope of ever seeing its tangible social results, Dr. Salazar pictures himself as the martyr "who was obliged to abandon the high calling of teaching and to tread a more difficult path with a heavier cross".[2]

[1] Salazar's speech to First Eucharistic Congress, Braga, 4.7.24.
[2] Foreword to *Discuros*, vol. II, Coimbra, 1939.

Although all historical evidence seems to suggest that the dictatorial path has only too often led to the martyrdom, under Police and censorship rules, not of the dictators but of those who dare to oppose them, Dr. Salazar has also stated: "Neither individual liberty, the greatest of all blessings, nor the interests of the people are better off in those countries which pride themselves on being democratic than in those under the rule of dictators."[1] Statements like these, which are bound to be encouraging news to the Russians, amongst others, not only led eventually to Dr. Salazar's intellectual discredit in Portugal, but have worried some Portuguese psychiatrists. Indeed, one of them is said to have stated that he could prove Dr. Salazar's insanity by the analysis of his speeches alone!

These speeches are of fundamental importance in the study of Portuguese contemporary politics, for they are the main source of the Estado Novo doctrines; but it should not be assumed that Dr. Salazar's use of his religious convictions is unanimously approved by Catholic intellectuals either in Portugal or elsewhere. He has often been taxed with inconsistency, and even charged with being a bad Catholic (when he engages, for instance, in elaborate distinctions between the individual and the person) by those who believe that the transcendental theological dogmas of Catholicism require a belief in a democratic form of society rather than in the hierarchical corporative state. Furthermore, under the eyes of the authorities, leaflets are distributed amongst the hundreds of thousands of pilgrims at Fatima (the Portuguese equivalent of Lourdes), suggesting that, in her reported apparitions to three little shepherds, the Blessed Virgin announced the "salvation" of Portugal for a time coinciding with the Salazar rule. This alone has provided an extreme example of the expediency of the dictator's religion.

In the manner of dictators, Dr. Salazar likes to expound in his speeches the basis of his political philosophy, and before going on to study the practical effects of his policies more closely it is illuminating to bear in mind the following quotations:

"The essential for the citizen of the *Estado Novo* is that he should have a clear-cut conception of his country and national unity; of the family as the social nucleus *par excellence*; of authority and those in authority; of spiritual values . . .; of the right to work; of the excellence of virtue and the sacred nature of religious beliefs."[2]

[1] Introduction, *Doctrine and Action*, Faber, London, 1939, p. 12.
[2] *Ibid.*, p. 26.

"We are opposed to all forms of internationalism, Communism, socialism, syndicalism and everything that may minimize or divide or break up the family . . ."[1]

"We are opposed to all the great heresies of today, all the more because we fail to see that any benefit has accrued through their propagation . . ."[2]

"We are anti-parliamentarians, anti-democrats, anti-liberals, and we are determined to establish a corporative state." [3]

[1] *Doctrine and Action*, p. 26.   [2] *Ibid.*, p. 26.   [3] *Ibid.*, p. 29.

Chapter II

THE CORPORATIVE STATE

The Swastika, the Fasces and the Caravels

THE FACT THAT the Government established by the *coup d'état* had no doctrine or programme provided Dr. Salazar with a unique opportunity to assert his own version of its original spirit. "Unless a *raison d'être* is found," he said, "there is nothing to be done but to re-establish the Constitution which has been suspended or violated since 1926." The threat implied in this statement found acceptance on the part of the ruling and ecclesiastical classes, who were preoccupied to welcome any measures designed to provide a positive political purpose and assure the continuity of an authoritarian regime.

Unlike Hitler, Mussolini or Franco, who had the support of organized parties or headed a political movement, Dr. Salazar, having come to power by force of circumstance, had to improvise and adapt his own traditionalist concepts which, ultra-nationalist as they were, were far from being entirely of Portuguese conception. The monarchic and Catholic philosophical background of "Corporativism" had penetrated into Portugal mainly through the writings of Antonio Sardinha, the originator of the doctrines of Luzitanian integralism. This was a literal translation into Portuguese language and thought of the doctrines expounded in France by Maurras and Daudet and their core of followers, who had organized the *Action Française* and influenced its subsequent Italian equivalent, *L'idea Nazionale*. In essence, in their ultimate form, these doctrines offered the organic and hierarchical concepts of the corporate character of mediaeval society as the alternative to what they considered to be the excessive individualism of the French Revolution, the mechanistic notions embodied in the Industrial Revolution, and the materialism and internationalism of Marxism and Leninism.

Realizing how behind Portuguese reaction was in the practical adaptation of corporativist ideologies, Dr. Salazar was the first to admit that the Government machine was not yet ready to put them into effect, and he set about to fill the doctrinal vacuum in gradual stages. On 30th July, 1930, in the presence of all the Cabinet Ministers, Dr. Salazar, disguised in the person of General Domingos de Oliveira, then Prime Minister, read the manifesto of the *Uniao Nacional* (National Union), the country's only legal political association, which, opposed to the party system, was not itself supposed to be called a party. It was in fact a loose coalition of "men of good will" who formed themselves into an unpopular front. Amongst the aims of the Union was that it should, apparently under a subsidiary *Centro de Estudos Politicos e Sociais* (Centre of Political and Social Studies), "present convenient and opportune suggestions aiming at the revision of certain juridical aspects [of Government] or methods of application". Never in political history had there been a more obvious example of an oligarchy, completely destitute of ideological justification, trying to find a purpose, a doctrine, to which to cling, if only to achieve some moral stand.

Dr. Salazar, the conscious or unconscious servant of the propertied and ecclesiastical classes, was then adding to his ministerial burden the study of the adaptation of the corporative system to the *Estado Novo* (the New State). Under this he was to reorganize Portuguese society by grouping the population, according to their respective activities, under compulsory corporations, syndicates and guilds, within the framework of the State's theoretical role as arbiter and guide. Emphasizing the totalitarian character of Corporativism (which suited the purposes of Fascism as an instrument of dictatorship), in addition to the economic corporations or councils, representing the employers' associations, trade unions, professional and provident societies, there were to be the moral corporations, representing the interests of religious bodies and philanthropic and humanitarian societies.

In the meantime, developing its policy of "social order", the Government promulgated the *Estatuto Nacional do Trabalho* (National Labour Statute), which put an end to the dangers that the reactionaries imagined they saw in the labour movements of the Socialists. These were movements that reached their heyday during the Republican period with the creation of the *Federacao Geral do Trabalho* (General Confederation of Labour), an association of the national syndicates which was responsible for the maintenance of Portuguese labour connections with international Socialist and Communist trade unions.

Dr. Salazar's utterances on the subject of the employment principles embodied in the *Estatuto* were a copy of the spirit, if not of the letter, of one of the key passages in the Italian Charter of Labour: "Since the private organization of production is a function of national concern . . . the employee is . . . an active collaborator in the enterprise, while its direction belongs to the employer, who also bears responsibility for it." In the process of making the worker an "active collaborator in the enterprise", which in any case he always was, the Dictatorship destroyed all socialist work done by a number of Portuguese Labour Congresses and the Labour daily newspaper (appropriately styled *A Batalha* —"The Battle"). Offered in its place was Dr. Salazar's pious concept: "If there are men whose only means of livelihood are derived from labour, we must face two conclusions: first that the national economy must be organized so that workers will have work to do; and secondly that the work shall be regulated and organized in such a way that the wages which men receive will be adequate to keep them."[1] For good measure, so that there should be no way of telling if the workers themselves regarded the wages as adequate, strikes became criminal offences and all workers were reduced to industrial serfdom.

In 1933 Dr. Salazar, having pressed quickly forward with the draft prepared by himself and his intimate collaborators, introduced the Constitution of the Corporative Republic and had it passed by general vote on lines similar to a plebiscite, but duly adapted to Portuguese circumstances. There were two major novel features of this voting system—the fact that the "No's" had to be written on the electoral ballot form in circumstances that assured the zealous watch of the police and of the hard core of fiercely voluntary or cheaply paid informers; and the remarkable criterion of counting abstentions as favourable votes: all in all, a practice that did not give much alternative to those voters who realized that their abstention would in any case only serve to leave a mark of suspicion attached to their undischarged names on the electoral roll.

This was indeed a disturbing start for a Constitution which promised in its Article 5: "The Portuguese State is a unitary and Corporative Republic, founded on the equality of the citizen before the law, and the free access of all classes to the benefits of civilization, and the participation of all structural elements of the nation in its administrative

[1] Speech, 16.3.33, at National Union headquarters.

life and in the enactment of the law". At the same time, however, the adoption of the Constitution was the first major blow to the credit of Dr. Salazar and his regime, since, historically, it exposed the flimsy structure of the whole legislative citadel, to be built, as it was, on words that lapsed into vagueness and deliberate ambiguity.

Conditioned by the trend of events in Europe, and particularly in neighbouring Spain, on whose political stability the survival of his regime would largely depend, in one of his typical "state of the regime" speeches the following year Dr. Salazar revealed the undercurrent of uncertainty among his followers: "Meanwhile we are advancing . . . Some, already satisfied with the happiness which flows from the heights of Tabor, say, 'It is better to rest here and build our tents upon this mountain'; others, preoccupied with the future, fearfully advise, 'Let us turn back'. Whatever the convenience of others may be, we must go forward."[1]

In the process of going forward, and in his determination to establish the reorganization of Portuguese society, Dr. Salazar gradually drifted, in spite of his repeated claim to the contrary, into a totalitarian regime, inspired by a totalitarian sense of mission. He was influenced and encouraged by the triumphs and might of National Socialism in Germany and the Fascist Party in Italy. Convinced that they would succeed in imposing a New Order which would last for a thousand years, he saw to it that he used Portugal's strategic position in relation to Spain to play his part in the historical contribution of international Fascism to Franco's war for power. In the process, he went far beyond just helping Franco, in terms of both military and economic aid. He established the habit of using Franco's execution squads for the discreet elimination of Portuguese socialists. His henchmen frequently handed them over, during the Spanish Civil War, to be included in the hosts of Spanish Republicans being slaughtered in bull rings not far from the Portuguese frontier.

After the consolidation of Franco's regime in Spain, Dr. Salazar's Estado Novo developed most of the basic characteristics of totalitarian states. He turned to Portuguese history to find the "virtues of the race" and the "colonizing mission of Portugal", which were his equivalents of the Nazi ideologies of Germanism and a special vocation towards the establishment of a new society and civilization. The swastikas, the fasces, the quinas and the caravels were essentially similar as ideological

[1] Speech, 28.4.34, Stock Exchange Palace, Oporto.

symbols. Salazar found in real or imagined British and international threats to Portuguese overseas possessions a way of feeding a peculiar xenophobic resentment against democratic countries. He had complete control of all means of armed force and rendered his enemies harmless through the agency of the Police and the Army. He adapted to Portuguese scale and conditions the aggressive and imperialist ambitions of Hitler and Mussolini towards the conquest of the world. "Through the designs of Providence by which the world is ruled," he said, "Portugal has no need of wars and conquests":[1] and, in fact, all it needed was to occupy effectively the untapped and scarcely populated Portuguese African territories. These provided Dr. Salazar with an outlet for his own imperialist tendencies, as well as ensuring for Portugal, according to his analysis of the economic and demographic situation, an equivalent of the "living space" of Fascist theory.

His New Era was awakening national conciousness. "The prestige of Portugal," he said, "will shine for ever . . . Everywhere the pride of being Portuguese will quicken the life-blood of the people and will vouchsafe peace and repose to the ashes of our heroes who are no longer with us. To reach our goal we have experienced a far-reaching revolution in economics, politics, ideas, customs, institutions, and in our collective life."[2] He displayed the utmost contempt for the interests and social problems of the African populations of Portuguese Africa, whom he completely ignored, in fact, in his public utterances on colonial policy. He took it for granted that these African wards would be under the rule and at the service of the national *Herrenvolk*—the settlers—the civilian agents of occupation in Portuguese African territories. Furthermore, he openly proclaimed his own concepts of racial superiority when, in one of his carefully prepared speeches, he referred to the Portuguese colonial peoples as "inferior races".[3]

Dr. Salazar turned his National Union into a hierarchically organized party, intertwined with a bureaucratic framework of government. Like the Nazi and Fascist parties, the bulk of the National Union membership formed a body of passive adherents who had answered Dr. Salazar's call for men willing to offer allegiance to the New Era. This body was in turn controlled by a hard core of ardent propagandists and police informers, not only belonging to the party but also organized

[1] Speech, 28.4.34.   [2] *Ibid.*
[3] Speech, 13.6.33, First Imperial Conference, on launching the Colonial Act.

into a militia, the *Legiao Portuguesa* (Portuguese Legion) and its branch, the *Defesa Civil do Territorio* (Territorial Civil Defence). These are both extremist organizations, which complement the regular police informers by voluntarily keeping a watch on individuals and institutions. The Legion members parade their green shirt uniforms up and down the country to show their readiness to defend the regime against hypothetical "forces of subversion", though these, even if existing, would at any rate be unarmed. The witch-hunting spirit that inspires all this seems, indeed, to imply that the mere fact that a man may eat meat on Fridays is evidence of Communist leanings.

Concerned with the transmission of National Union ideologies and political power to the younger generations, Dr. Salazar called in German Hitler Youth experts, who not only helped to organize his own Youth Movement, but were responsible for the introduction of essentially similar methods in primary and secondary education. The State, and no one else, in Dr. Salazar's opinion, has the right "to promote, to harmonize and to control all national activities; to teach the younger generation to be devoted to their country, to instil discipline into them, to encourage them to practise sports and physical exercises, so that they may be trained for greater activity and be ready to do anything that might be demanded in the national interest and by the national honour."[1]

To complete the control of the nation, Dr. Salazar was using the State Security Police (*Policia Internacional e de Defesa do Estado*, PIDE for short) whose secret branch had close technical connections with the Gestapo and adopted all its modern methods of political control. In the same pattern, it was ultimately linked directly with the Dictator through a trusted core of lieutenants, who commanded a high measure of independent and arbitrary powers, often arresting moderate dissident members of the regime's own, or patronised, political and religious organizations *pour encourager les autres*. Under special laws, they could arrest any citizen and confine him to imprisonment in special political jails, for "investigation", for consecutive periods of three months, usually with no other purpose than repression. The real or assumed extent of their organization, and their reputation for the actual use of modern scientific, physical and psychological methods of handling political prisoners (who often committed suicide, or were physically and mentally ruined) added to their efficiency as a repressive

[1] Speech, 30.6.30, at the Council of State.

force. Far from being a passive body, the PIDE, like the Gestapo and the Italian Police, is supplied with a large number of informers and agents who specialize in infiltrating the ranks of identifiable opposition groups at all levels of organization, while individuals are watched in every sphere of public and private activity.

In the field of mass communication Dr. Salazar achieved total control, not only by means of imposing censorship of the Press ("Newspapers," he said, "are the spiritual food of the people, and like all foods must be controlled"), but by gradually gaining complete power over radio, cinema and television. The subservient cadres of the National Union spread throughout most editorial bodies of supposedly independent papers completed the Government's monopoly of the Press.

In order to build an "island of separateness" (in the manner of the Fascist regimes), or a "curtain" (as favoured by Communist dictatorships), he created the National Information Secretariat, and sponsored "independent" news agencies. These had a complete monopoly of news services between Portuguese territories, which therefore became further "islands of separateness" in their turn. The efficiency of the Police rule, the language barrier, the fact that, politically, the country had become a mere appendage to the Spanish regime, as well as the control of visiting foreign journalists, lead to the almost complete impenetrability of Portugal and its overseas territories to world public opinion.

In addition, Dr. Salazar gained central direction of the country's economy ("The nation as an economic unit is subject to the State") through the framework of social and economic control provided by the corporative organization. The key posts in both the employers' guilds, covering practically all branches of economic activity, on the one hand, and the employees' syndicates, the *Casas do Povo* (People's Houses, for the rural population) and *Casas dos Pescadores*, (Fishermen's Houses), on the other, were filled by Government supporters. In the process, the State became the preserve of plutocracy. While the Constitution laid down that the State should prevent "the excessive profits of capital", and provided for the appointment of Government delegates to the country's major companies and enterprises to enforce this, these delegates not only came to arrangements with the company directors, but often exchanged their role of delegates for that of managing directors themselves. Furthermore, in order to ensure an identity of interests between the rich industrialists and the senior civil servants and Army officials, qualification for selection as a Government delegate was dependent on either Army rank or political influence inside the National Union. By engaging in comparatively vast Development Plans (which would better be defined as public works programmes, for they consist mainly in the execution of engineering projects aimed at "honouring" the nation), and by the allocation of such things as building materials to those companies which saw to it that their management boards were made up of prominent "nationalists" and deputies of the "National Assembly", the Government could continually distribute patronage in the form of high executive positions and wealth.

A policy of partnership between the State and private enterprise was deliberately pursued. It appears that Portuguese capital refrains from venturing into business unless investments are assured of absolute security and profits. To reach this objective the Government includes in the Development Plans, as items for industrial development, huge sums which are incorporated into the capital of semi-public companies. The private partners of the regime thus have the assurance of Government protection for their capital investment. Monopoly concessions and other privileges are granted to these companies, and profits are accordingly kept at a generously rewarding level. Most Portuguese Ministers and other senior Government officials are associated with the country's biggest industries. Overseas Ministers are often seconded from the Chairmanship of a body such as the *Banco Nacional Ultramarino* or the Bank of Angola (the issuing banks for the Portuguese Empire). Former governors of African territories frequently sit on the boards of major overseas concerns. Ministers of Economic Affairs have used their term of office to protect their own businesses, which, in some cases, play a big part in the national economy.

Totalitarianism in Portugal has, of course, distinctive features of its own. Dr. Salazar could not possibly identify his regime with the atheism of the Nazis, and he often criticized Mussolini for socialist tendencies. The country's religious and cultural traditions form an important background to concepts of purely Portuguese application.

Dr. Salazar himself is known to be a man of austere habits and has kept immune from the infection of *tubaronismo*, a term derived from the Portuguese word for shark, and currently applied to the voracious appetite of the Portuguese oligarchy. He has declared that he "owes to Providence the grace of being poor" (although one could add that he did not need to spend his own money when buying himself political power). Yet, under his regime, showing a remarkable lack of solidarity with those who share to an even greater extent in this grace of being poor, such signs as É proíbido mendigar ("Begging is Forbidden") are placed in areas frequented by rich tourists, where, incidentally, beggars would be most likely to do any business.

Tight Reins and Blinkers

It is not even completely clear whether some of the Estado Novo men, including Dr. Salazar, are fully aware of the nature of their own theories. Those who only know their own countries and people usually end up as the victims of their own parochialism and lack a sense of proportion. Dr. Salazar often mentions foreign writers and journalists in his speeches, as if being French, British or American were necessarily an intellectual qualification. And Mr. Costa Brochado, none other than a leading member of the Executive of the National Union, refers to Dr. Salazar in this vein: "With the laying down of the National Union, Salazar embarked on the great political task of our time by creating the New State, a marvel of political philosophy and constitutional law, which was to make him, in the political history of the present, one of the greatest figures of all time . . . The mission of statesmen like Salazar, true guides of mankind who have already been called in France the 'special envoys of Providence', is not to alter the laws of nature but to live in the minds and spirits of their collaborators."[1] Others, like the leader of the Women's Catholic League, go about claiming that in Fatima "Our Lady wished to speak to the men of today. This fact makes us the people primarily responsible for the salvation of the world. It was not, as some believe, a proof of preference or a reward. It was a mission entrusted to us. Why? God knows why."[2]

Then there are a number of philosophers, usually members of the well-fed middle and upper classes, who rationalize and expound the centuries-old poverty of the Portuguese people as if it were a deliberate matter of choice: "One of our hopes is that we may be permitted to be poor, while we appear to be rich, and to be rich while we appear

---

[1] National Union sponsored lecture, January 1960.

[2] Portugal (Secretariado Nacional de Informacao, Lisbon), January/February 1960.

to be poor, and that no one lay covetous hands upon the wealth we possess on the grounds that it does not make us rich. We do not wish to be rich—we wish to live—which is something richer. Trade and industry are the sources of an ostentatious wealth which may mislead the *nouveaux riches* but does not deceive the old poor . . . Man seeks the shining gold and finds it only in his work, unpretentious though that work might be. Our colonial tradition, is that of a poverty that has enriched the world and made it fertile."[1] There is no way of telling where deliberate mystification of others begins or self-deception ends. Historical reverie is stimulated by an almost permanent programme of Centennial commemorations, as if the Estado Novo were afraid to face the present and the future. Leaping back over hundreds of years, the retrospection is almost exclusively devoted to the fifteenth-century discoveries. This nostalgia for the long, long ago can do as little to solve the dramatic political and social problems of the country as the current practice of arresting beggars, or prohibiting their circulation in tourist resorts, can do towards solving the problems of their misery.

---

[1] Dr. Agostinho Campos in a colonial address. Quoted by F. Egerton in *Salazar, Rebuilder of Portugal*, Hodder & Stoughton Ltd., 1943, p. 275.

CHAPTER III

THE ESTADO NOVO AND THE PORTUGUESE PEOPLE

Behind the Economic Façade

WHILE ILLITERACY AND semi-literacy keep the people plunged in ignorance of the most elementary socio-economic facts, and censorship and repressive legislation prevent the educated minority from any form of public discussion and analysis of the basic problems confronting their country, the Portuguese rulers cannot rely exclusively on the protection provided by its legislation and its police. Many superficial changes in twentieth-century Portugal have been introduced under the influence of Portugal's inevitable external relationships, rather than as the result of pressures of a domestic nature.

Portugal's geographical position in a highly developed continent constantly increases the contrast between Portuguese conditions and those of other countries. It is evident from the study of the Estado Novo's economic and social policies that Portugal has not undergone the process of democratic evolution, or revolution, that has changed the patterns of society in practically all other European countries. The Portuguese ruling class maintains its traditional position of political power, and the Estado Novo has gradually come under the control of the old royalist families. Don Juan, the pretender to the Spanish throne, once commented that "while Spain is a monarchy where it is dangerous to be a monarchist, Portugal is a Republic where it is dangerous to be a republican".

Currently the socio-economic policies of the Estado Novo reveal its political nature. Behind a murky façade of technological progress lie hidden the real facts of the structure of Portuguese society. The revenue of the Portuguese Government is only fourteen per cent of the gross national output, as compared with thirty per cent in Great Britain and France, twenty-nine per cent in Germany, twenty-eight per cent in the United States, twenty-seven per cent in Sweden and

Austria. In short, it is the lowest in Europe (including Greece, reputedly an underdeveloped nation, where the equivalent figure is twenty per cent). As expressed in the national budget, the following are the main items of expenditure:

Ordinary Expenditure (in million escudos)

				Education	Health and Social Assistance	Defence
1960	..	..	..	957	615	1,419
1961	..	..	..	1,015	653	1,458

Extraordinary Expenditure

1960	..	..	..	—	—	799
1961	..	..	..	—	—	1,656
				1,972	1,268	5,332

The contrast between defence expenditure and expenditure on social assistance, health and education, is not a new feature of the Estado Novo's administrative policies, although it obviously reflects the increasing demands caused by unrest in Portuguese Angola and Mozambique, where, over the past few years, there has been a corresponding and complementary increase in military expenditure in the respective budgets of both territories themselves. Defence absorbed some forty per cent of all public expenditure in Portugal in the period 1935–1950 and was consistently at a level with health, social assistance and education put together. This alone reveals the position of the armed forces as the mainstay of the regime. Portugal ranks at the United Nations as one of the greatest upholders of such a cause as anti-disarmament, and the Portuguese Government has expressed its fears over the possible consequences of scientific warfare on the disarmament question. The maintenance of conventional armies has been defended by the Portuguese Delegate, Dr. Vasco Garin, in an historic speech in which he seriously advanced the idea that there should be unanimity of military purpose between the Western and the Soviet blocs on earth, on account of a possible inter-planetary war. That this speech met with the approval of Dr. Salazar is shown by the fact that Dr. Garin is still the head of the Portuguese Delegation, in spite of a number of protests raised at the time by some prominent Estado Novo men.

An essential characteristic of the Estado Novo's development policy is what is termed in Portugal *desenvolvimento de fachada* (façade development). The fact that economic development in Portugal has been mainly directed towards urban and public works cannot be easily dismissed in terms of economic criteria. It is a feature deeply associated with the nature of the Portuguese regime. It aims on the one hand at propaganda for the administration: visible development is more convincing than the release of statistical data which could hardly be understood by the majority of Portuguese people. On the other hand, it covers a need to mystify visitors to Portugal. Foreign tourism from European countries and the United States is an increasingly important source of revenue and international goodwill. Lisbon and its tourist surroundings have been turned into Portugal's visiting-room, while a network of *Pousadas*, the Portuguese equivalent of motels, combining modern comfort with scenery and the best of Portuguese food and tradition, gives the tourist an excellent first impression of the country, and often misleads otherwise liberal-minded visitors. A system of clean, modern roads links Portugal's main tourist attractions, and much of the road development under the Estado Novo is essentially associated with tourism, as in the specific case of a modern highway between Lisbon airport and the Estoril resort. Hydro-electric dams, bridges, sports stadiums, hospitals and school buildings are frequently included in the programme of visits for foreign personalities.

Commenting on the enthusiasm of Brazilian tourists, Mr. Alvaro Lins, former Brazilian Ambassador in Lisbon says in his book *Mission to Portugal*:[1] "Brazilians visiting Portugal for brief periods are not authorized to judge Portuguese life. A sensitive and humanitarian Brazilian living permanently in Portugal . . . sees the mark of dictatorship and police terror on the faces of the Portuguese. Their tormented expressions reflect demoralization, revolt, often despair and always intranquillity, insecurity and fear. Fear of unemployment, fear of prison. . . . The same phenomenon is visible in the country, in areas where collective life is not on the show-window pattern of Lisbon and Oporto. The tourist . . . is often heard to exclaim: Magnificent roads! Well cultivated fields! How these workers produce and how well organized they are! . . . But a Brazilian who knows the reality knows what is behind and beyond this façade. He knows that none of these things belongs to the Portuguese people; he knows that

[1] *Missao em Portugal*, Editora Civilizaçao Brasileira SA, Rio de Janeiro, 1960.

these things belong on the contrary to a handful of rich bankers and feudal landlords, to a small group of men who control the reins of political power. This group is formed by prosperous business men who hold monopolies and who are engaged in the pursuit of official prestige and the amassing of quick fortunes; who receive the sanction of the State in their dubious transactions—the very group which forms the inner court of, and pander to, the little Spanish-inquisitor-cum-dictator . . . [To comment] on Portuguese life one needs to know that in the fields of Alemtejo there are men and women who earn two shillings a day, and even then can only work three days a week, since there is only work available for half of the Alemtejo's slaves of the soil."

Statistical data clearly show that expenditure on public works, both by the Government and through Government-controlled municipal budgets, has been effected at the cost of savings on social assistance and education. More than fifty per cent of Portugal's labour force lives in a state of under-employment, while the bulk of the population anyhow lives at subsistence levels; yet the Government's current expenditure on health services is less than fifteen shillings a year per head of the population. In consequence, Portugal's health statistics are obviously significant of social standards—in point of fact, it is in the field of medical assistance that the cultural traits acquired through a centuries-old situation of social poverty are best revealed: the practice of providing medical assistance out of personal charity is widespread in Portugal. Doctors, mostly belonging to richer families, count amongst their clients a majority of non-payers and slow payers, and often give away samples of pharmaceutical products. The intake of calories by the Portuguese people is one of the lowest in Europe and is equal to that of Tunisia or the Belgian Congo. Compared with 102 other countries, where the mortality rate among children up to one year does not exceed fifty per one thousand, Portugal's rate is eighty-eight. In 1960, infant mortality rates were more than twice those in Czechoslovakia, Japan or Singapore. Sixty per cent of births in Portugal take place without the help of either a doctor or a midwife. The incidence of tuberculosis remains one of the highest in Europe.

But it is perhaps in the field of education that the nature of Portuguese Government is demonstrated most plainly. With Portugal's current rate of illiteracy at over forty per cent, the following is a comparative list of the number of primary, secondary and technical students enrolled in 1958 in a selected number of countries with populations varying from three to ten million people, as indicated in brackets:

	Pre-school	Primary	Secondary	Technical	Total Sec. & Techn.
Portugal (9)	4,820	841,422	76,637	64,977	141,614
Netherlands (10·5) ..	361,936	1,519,952	330,170	202,937	533,107
Belgium (9)	362,562	874,586	248,914	283,053	531,967
Norway (3·5)		447,250	49,102	44,459	93,561
Sweden (7)		885,000	199,390	47,782	247,172
Switzerland (5) ..		548,875	125,957	7,682	133,639
Denmark (4·4) ..		519,931	133,489	56,266	189,755

Not only is the number of primary school students proportionately lower in Portugal, but Portuguese figures include adults who are currently enrolled in rudimentary education programmes so that they can, on knowing little more than how to sign their names, decrease the appalling illiteracy figures released to UNESCO and other international organizations. Moreover, the table shows that Portuguese education is mostly confined to primary school. Enrolment to secondary education is restricted by many social factors, and some thirty per cent of technical students are night pupils. For one thing, most Portuguese children start working in their early teens, as parents can hardly spare them more time, let alone provide the clothing, school books, material and fees required for the socially exclusive Lyceums. As for university education, only the upper classes can afford either the time or the expenditure, with the result that the selection of Portuguese intelligence is restricted to a small minority, and the type of education, largely dependent on the whim of rich parents, ceases to be adapted to socio-economic needs. In 1957 there were 3,318 students studying philosophy and philology, and 1,229 studying law; in the same year the number of engineering students was 474, and these included the civil engineering, electrical and mechanical branches. Although veterinary surgeons and agricultural engineers are obviously needed in a predominantly agrarian empire, there were in 1957 only some twenty graduations in veterinary science and sixty graduations in agronomy, as compared with 282 graduates in philosophy and 170 graduates in theology in the high ecclesiastical institutions of the country.

A statistical comparison between Portugal and Norway, for instance, reveals (a) that non-colonialist Norway has a national income forty per cent higher than that of Portugal, with less than forty per cent of the Portuguese population; (b) that its national budget is currently twenty-three per cent of the national income as compared with Portugal's fourteen per cent; (c) that transfer payments, insurance benefits and subsidies are six times the Portuguese total, or more than twelve times as great on a *per capita* rate; (d) that Norwegian social security payments are nine per cent of the national income, as compared with Portugal's three per cent; (e) that capital accumulation is twenty-nine per cent of the national income as compared with Portugal's sixteen per cent; (f) that the current number of houses built in Norway is on a level with Portugal's (an average of some thirty thousand houses per year) in spite of the less acute housing problem and a population of only some 3,500,000 people as compared with Portugal's nine million; and (g) that Norway lives happily without a large Army, an empire or a State Police, and its people can freely read and write for the country's daily Press.

What Tourists do not See

In a country where four of the greatest landlords between them own 235,000 acres of land, the same acreage as is owned by 50,400 small farmers, the pattern of socio-economic development is patently circumstantial and unbalanced. Socially and technologically Portugal has no uniform age. While jet propulsion planes land at Lisbon, and Lisbon hotels and rich houses have all the comforts and gadgets of modern civilization, in the Northern district of Tras dos Montes the rural population still lives in mediaeval style, bartering its commodities and, in isolated centres, hardly participating in a money economy. Side by side with modern main roads and beyond the visual range of foreign tourists, the rural population throughout most of Portugal still uses the Roman ox-cart and primitive methods of cultivation. Their decaying stone houses are utterly without comfort. Electricity, when available, cannot be afforded. The average annual earnings of some rural workers can be estimated at fifty to seventy pounds. This explains the fact that the annual consumption of electric current in Portugal is fifteen kws per head, as compared with an average among OEEC countries of one hundred.

Using tommy-guns, the dictator's troops enforce the expropriation of communal land in the mountains, depriving those who have not a single square inch of land or a tree of their own of the use of neglected mountain land for cattle grazing and gathering wood for the family fire. Between 1938 and 1951, according to the archives of the *Registo Predial* (the land Registry) more than half a million small farms were incorporated into big estates.

In the region of Abrantes, as in many other areas of Portugal, rural workers queue up in the mornings in desperate need to be included in the landlord's daily selection of seasonal labour, often for wages as low as four shillings a day. If they are weak or sick or unlucky, for lack of any social assistance they will have to eat nothing but a bare piece of maize bread and sardines. In Alemtejo, where most of the larger family estates are concentrated, the current wages are so low, even by Portuguese standards, that the *Guarda Republicana*, or rural police, often have to force men and women to carry out their work at gun-point. The niceties of labour legislation are beyond their comprehension, strikes are considered a crime, but stoppages are spontaneous movements of revolt against misery and inequality. With daily wages ranging from two shillings for women and five shillings for men, most rural workers live at a meagre level of subsistence and it is not surprising that the only reported cases of trachoma and other poverty diseases long curbed or eliminated in Europe have been found amongst them. Along the coast of Portugal, fishermen still use mediaeval rowing-boats or small unsafe trawlers, and the frequent night tragedies in which they vanish at sea while their women and children cry on the beaches excite the imagination of national dramatists more than they move many a well-fed and fish-loving member of the Portuguese Government.

These poor people, the rural and fishing population, live or exist within a small walking-distance world. Mostly illiterate, they often resist the Government mandates pertaining to primary education and force their children to help them as workers rather than send them to school—a fact that is often misinterpreted as the reflection of their character, instead of as a consequence of the extreme misery of their upbringing. They recognize intuitively that education in the circumstances is unrelated to their socio-economic standards, when a daily newspaper costs threepence, the price of half a dozen sardines.

For lack of theatres or cinemas, their only entertainments are the "romarias", religious festivities around neighbouring churches where small markets selling regional dishes and fancy religious goods are a source of income for the local church. In richer "romarias" musical bands provide amusement and, at the same time, a pretext for the meeting of sexes. In the mountains some people go years without seeing a train. Unable to afford the threepence charged for coffee, or without clothes which would meet with the management's standards, they watch coffee-bar television screens from the street, sometimes in the cold and the rain, hoping to see their sports heroes playing soccer, or the roller-skating contests in distant Lisbon and Oporto towns. Apart from this, their daily routine is work, from sunrise to sundown and for such people a visit to Lisbon, Oporto, Fatima or some seaside resort where bigger "romarias" are staged is an experience of a life-time.

For industrial workers, the average daily wage in Portugal is some 6s.3d. *per day* of work, compared with an average of 6s. *per hour* in Sweden, Denmark and Norway. Although this comparison should be accepted with some reservations to allow for differences in the cost of living, the fact is that Portugal's figure is the total gross wage, while Scandinavian averages are not only many times higher in absolute terms and purchasing power, but are exclusive of social security and assistance benefits, which are practically non-existent in Portugal. For employees in the fish canneries, the average is only 4s.3d. As rents in the larger towns vary from £3 to £10 a month, the price of a man's suit from £8 to £15, and with meat at 4s. a pound and an average cinema ticket 2s. 6d., industrial workers and their families are obviously under-housed, under-clothed, under-fed and under-educated. In fact, conditions prevailing in the Portuguese working-class are below the level of those prevailing amongst people living with the aid of national assistance, retirement, illness or unemployment bene-fit in the more socially advanced countries of Europe.

In spite of harsh measures to maintain the cost of living at an adequately low level (at the expense of the rural and fishing populations who supply the food), real wages dropped by a third between 1939 and 1958. No Lisbon worker is able to build his own home, for lack of the minimum funds to qualify for Government help. In Lisbon alone, thirty-one thousand families have no home of their own and share their over-crowded dwellings with others. Eleven thousand families live in dwellings unfit for human habitation, and these include some buildings on the Government's own housing-estates on the outskirts of Lisbon and Oporto, put up as a measure of social relief to replace the worst of the urban slums.

Though it would be misleading to suggest that Portugal no longer has an intellectual *élite*, one sad result of these appalling social conditions is that emigration continues to attract a high proportion of the country's best brains and manpower, even after thirty-five years of the Estado Novo's "economic revolution". Emigration to Brazil, and on a smaller scale to practically every place in the world, is a social phenomenon of which the significance goes beyond that expressed by statistical data. Emigration, like the national lottery and the sad *fado* song, is a cultural trait: the average educated or uneducated Portuguese is either hoping to emigrate, or connected through the family with emigrants, or regretting his inability to emigrate. Shipping lines specializing in carrying emigrants have adapted their third-class deck accommodation and catering services to relatively low fares, but, even so, most prospective passengers can hardly afford them. The fact that unskilled Portuguese applicants do not meet with either the regulations or the preference of the immigration authorities of most industrialized countries is another deterrent. Nevertheless, from 1951 to 1960, over 350,000 people, or nearly half the total population increase during the same period, left Portugal to settle, for the most part, in Brazil. Emphasizing the social factors involved, some ninety per cent of the total number of emigrants were men travelling alone. The effects of their absence are felt in many Portuguese areas, such as Minho, where there are both a chronic labour shortage and a great number of broken homes and families.

CHAPTER IV

THE WORLD WAR AND THE COLD WAR

Dr. Goebbels Speaks the Truth

IN HISTORICAL PERSPECTIVE, Portugal's separation from Spain as a national entity is partly due to the implications of the centuries-old Anglo-Portuguese Alliance. The original purpose of this Alliance has been strengthened since the nineteenth century by a number of close new political and economic connections. In modern history the United Kingdom has had the most important share in Portugal's foreign trade, and a large stake in the control and ownership of some major Portuguese economic activities, such as the Port Wine and export businesses, and modern public services, as, for instance, telephones and tramways in both Lisbon and Oporto. A partner in Portuguese colonialism in Africa, British capital has a variety of interests in Portuguese Angola and Mozambique, in concerns ranging from railways, mining, sugar plantations and shipping to clearing agencies and banking. Moreover, landlocked British African territories have specially close economic relationships, with Mozambique. Apart from neighbouring Spain and distant Brazil, Great Britain has therefore been the most important factor in Portuguese foreign policy.

How Great Britain has managed to accommodate her democratic tradition to her political relationships with Fascist Portugal is one of the greatest paradoxes of international diplomacy. To this day, for instance, it is not very clear, at any rate to Portuguese democrats, what a British Army commission, set up during the Spanish Civil War at the invitation of Dr. Salazar's Government itself, was doing on the Portuguese-Spanish frontier. Ostensibly it was there to prevent the infringement of regulations embodied in the non-intervention policy, to which both countries subscribed. Since not only military aid but even the persons of Portuguese democrats are known to have been exported to Spain at the time, one can only conclude that the Commission must have been enjoying a very good brand of tea or Port wine (probably supplied by the Salazar regime in the interests of Anglo-Portuguese friendship) while it amiably kept watch on the wrong parts of the frontier.

When Great Britain later became one of the major victims of Nazi and Fascist warfare, Anglo-Portuguese diplomatic relations went on as usual. Admittedly, Dr. Salazar was genuinely anxious to keep Portugal out of the war, and the Allies themselves were not willing to complicate matters even further by having the Iberian Peninsula overrun by the Nazi armies (they knew tacitly that, at least in the first stages of the war, the Franco and Salazar political machines would have provided the Nazis with a powerful and strategically placed fifth column). The historical fact is, however, that during the war, ideologically and politically, Spain and Portugal were extensions of the territory that was occupied by the Third Reich.

One needs only to read the war diaries of the Nazi leaders to understand how useful as German intelligence outposts must have been the work of Dr. Salazar's diplomatic services in Great Britain, of German diplomatic missions in Lisbon, and of consular services in Portuguese Africa, mainly in the busy port of Lourenço Marques. Nazi Germany had every reason to approve the friendly neutrality of Dr. Salazar, particularly as it could get the only valuable strategic mineral raw materials it needed from Portugal. Dr. Goebbels, who, in his private *Diaries*, secretly indulged in the cult of truth, often referred to important information just received from London, via Lisbon, and has even an enigmatic reference to a speech by Dr. Salazar, delivered to a "small group" and "not released for general use", whereby he (Dr. Goebbels) was happy to conclude that "as long as Dr. Salazar remains in power nothing really hostile to us [the Nazis] will be done".

When the trend of the war changed and, in October 1943, Dr. Salazar was forced to comply, against the will of the rabid Fascist wing of his clique, with the cession to the Allies of military bases in the Atlantic islands of the Azores, Dr. Salazar's decision was seen by many a prominent Nazi leader as yet another betrayal in the ranks of international Fascism. In order to justify his change of heart—and much to the bitter amusement of the Nazi leaders—Dr. Salazar supported Franco's proposal to make Spain and Portugal, linked by their own Iberian Bloc pact, the surviving bastions of Western values and Christianity. Dr. Goebbels, summing up the situation in his entry for the 13th November, 1943, wrote: "I have received a detailed report about the situation in Portugal. From it the following can be gathered. Salazar is undoubtedly the master of Portugal, but he relies on his armed forces. Unfortunately he has lost his faith in us [the Nazis] to some extent, and therefore keeps swaying to and fro between the extremes of the pendulum. The same is true of Franco. The dictators would do far better if they openly took sides with us, for if our side does not win they are lost anyway."

Dr. Salazar indeed welcomed the end of the war in a rather gloomy and funereal mood, for in 1945 he was, with de Valera of the Irish Republic, the only head of State to send his regrets to Grand Admiral Doenitz on the death of Chancellor Hitler. The appalling nature and extent of that Hitlerian nightmare, the New Order, under which millions of people vanished, now stood plainly revealed: yet, placing diplomatic "respectability" above any other moral consideration, Dr. Salazar went one better than many of the Nazi leaders themselves, some of whom had conspired against the life of their Führer, and ordered the flag of Portugal to be flown at half-mast.

The Portuguese people had different views, and the emotion with which *they* celebrated the end of the war carried the hope of their own freedom from dictatorship. Dr. Salazar's arguments that a time of war was not exactly suitable for effecting any major change in the Portuguese political situation were no longer valid. It had seemed to them that the victory of democracy would bring about the big moment of reckoning for his regime, in whose ranks were all the big business men who had profited from the supply of raw materials and foodstuffs to the Axis during hostilities. There was talk of a massive "black list" in the British and American embassies, containing the names of these people, and reports on the volume of their business and the degree of their responsibility for the policy of collaborationist neutrality pursued by the Salazar regime.

Rather hopefully, a group of Portuguese democrats tried to animate the dull Portuguese political scene by setting up an "opposition" movement, demanding "free elections, revision of the electoral rolls, amnesty of political prisoners and freedom of the Press". All that a citizen was required to do was to sign his name on one of the lists that were being circulated throughout the country. When hundreds of thousands of democrats had answered the "opposition" call, the Government suddenly decided that things were going a bit too far for its taste, and took a peculiar step: it called the whole thing "anti-constitutional", and had some of the most active promoters arrested so that they (mostly lawyers) could discuss with the police the niceties of legislative interpretation. Moreover, the Government seized the lists. The fact that most subscribers had in good faith signed their names and addresses as legibly as possible gave the Government a splendid opportunity to turn the registers into a sort of police census of the democratic population. Dr. Salazar then ordered the police to select the names of senior government dependents who, on the spur of the moment, had thought they were living under a Christian regime. A slow, discreet but ruthless purge followed. Prominent Portuguese professors, senior civil servants and school-teachers were either summarily dismissed or forced to choose between retracting their attitude and facing unemployment—for dismissal in Portugal, where the Government is the most important single employer in the educational field, means inevitable ruin.

There were two main factors responsible for the continued immunity of Dr. Salazar. At home, his personal dictatorship had become inextricably embodied in the National Union dictatorship, and the armed forces, big business and the Catholic Church had a vested interest in maintaining the *status quo*: the administrative apparatus, supported by thousands of collaborationists and dependents, had in fact acquired a momentum of its own, and the interested parties were determined to perpetuate the regime, even if the circumstances that had favoured its establishment no longer subsisted. The Republican issue was dead, and the Communist issue was for the meantime to become the *raison d'être* of the Estado Novo. Love of freedom, passionate and widespread as it was, could not hope to match the instinct of self-preservation displayed by those who were looking with apprehension at the hard mood of the people's courts in post-war Europe. The other factor was the post-war international situation, which, contrary to all expectations, had not turned out to be unfavourable to Dr. Salazar, though he had many anxious moments, as at the time of the change of government in Britain, when he sadly commented on the ingratitude of the British people towards their leader, Churchill.

Dr. Salazar had already been engaged in a reassessment of his regime's survival problems as far back as June 1942. In a speech made at this time, concluding that "it was an exaggeration to believe that Great Britain wished to favour the growth of Communism in Europe", and commenting on the enormous task of reconstruction that would fall to the victors, he added: "No one can suppose that such a task, which will call for decades of intensive work, brotherly collaboration and mutual understanding both within each nation and without, can be carried on in the conditions of political, economic and social disorder into which Europe was thrown as a result of the previous war."[1]

In point of fact he was right: the Allies, their hands full of troubles and problems, ranging from Soviet expansionism to the readjustment of their economies and the economies of the countries devastated by the war, had neither time nor interest to review their policies towards the Spanish and Portuguese governments. But British and American attitudes were to be judged, by Portuguese people, on the actions of their respective diplomatic services in Lisbon. The principles of "brotherly collaboration" were apparently being taken to heart. Apart from reading the Government abstract of statistics, American and British diplomats went around cultivating the friendship of the rich and sociable Portuguese and those local British and American business men who are always ready to confirm that Dr. Salazar is a benevolent despot. In the process, they became ineffective as diplomatic representatives and were a discredit to the democratic values proclaimed by their countries. The Portuguese people in general are indeed too poor for social gatherings; however, when they saw that the "black lists" were apparently being used as the basis of guest-lists for post-war diplomatic parties, they began to think that British love of democracy must, at least at Government levels, be kept for domestic consumption. It seemed as though many a British politician released the frustrations of socialism at home by patronizing reactionary causes abroad. As for the reputation of America, many Portuguese felt that the Statue of Liberty was betrayed from the day President Roosevelt died. They had come to the conclusion that the protection of democracy and of small oppressed peoples had been rather a reflection of the character of a great President than a consistent line of national policy.

The over-simplification of the political scene as viewed from London and Washington seemed to be that Portugal, being a small country, would have to turn West, even if Salazar were to fall. The grievances

[1] Broadcast on Defence. *Discursos*, vol. III, p. 348.

of the peasants, the discontent of the middle classes were amply concealed by the Portuguese socialites who went around the embassies trying to forget, amidst laughter and drinks, the realities of their country's economic and social conditions. That British, American and even Portuguese diplomats should all have closed their eyes to the fact that Portugal was simultaneously one of the most backward nations in Europe and the owner of the third largest colonial Empire in the world: that they should have failed to see the explosive situation that must one day expose the fair-weather nature of their diplomatic connections, is proof that British and American foreign policy was unwise indeed in this post-war period.

Forgotten in the War of War Memoirs

Constantly absorbed by fresh emergencies in distant areas of Asia or the Middle East, its political studies confined almost exclusively to a new war of war memories, public opinion in the West remained largely oblivious of the trend of Anglo-American policy towards the Iberian Peninsula. Foreign correspondents could find little to report in the monotony of life under the Salazar dictatorship and failed to grasp the long-term significance of apparently isolated and remote political incidents.

When the picturesque dispute over the Goan issue reached the headlines in 1954, many a student of Portuguese affairs also failed to recognize that Mr. Nehru was for some years to be the unknowing leader of the Portuguese struggle for freedom, or that Goa itself would be the starting point of Dr. Salazar's decline. However, Portuguese democrats knew that the orphan of Nazism and Fascism could hardly apply to his relations with genuinely democratic countries his own naïve and arrogant blend of political principles.

According to the Salazar Government's only official statement on the issues involved, Mr. Nehru had dared to press claims for the peaceful political settlement of an illogical situation. This was the anachronistic oddity of leaving under the rule of a European country 1,542 square miles of separated enclaves in Goa, south of Bombay, and Damao and Diu, north of Bombay, together inhabited by some 700,000 people, at a time when the British had just ended their rule over the remaining 1,143,267 square miles and its 400,000,000 people. Dr. Salazar claimed that Mr. Nehru knew very little about international law. Mr. Nehru, for his part, hardly knew how best to handle the "mediaeval political chevalier" that Dr. Salazar was turning out to be. For good measure, and tired of the endless and tricky diplomatic proceedings, Mr. Nehru decided that diplomatic relations between the two countries should be suspended.

The Portuguese people were at first so busy thinking about their own political, economic and social problems that they had little time to notice that nothing had been said by Dr. Salazar about the nature of these Indo-Portuguese negotiations, or, for that matter, about the "satyagraha" which had taken place as far back as 1946, when thirteen Goan leaders became the first of their people to be the "guests" of the Portuguese PIDE in Lisbon. However, the Goa question was gradually to acquire, largely owing to Dr. Salazar's obstinacy, an importance in Portuguese politics far out of proportion to its material significance.

Democratic leaders in Portugal did not allow themselves to be misled for long by Government propaganda. The uniformity of the rule of the Estado Novo undoubtedly extended to far away Goa. Though Portuguese democrats were of course not informed of this, none other than the world-respected humanist Mahatma Gandhi, in a letter to the Governor-General of Goa on 2nd August, 1946, had commented: " . . . What I see and know of the condition of things in Goa is hardly edifying. That the Indians in Goa have been speechless is proof not of the innocence or the philanthropic nature of the Portu-guese Government, but of the rule of terror. You will forgive me for not subscribing to your statement that there is full liberty in Goa and that the agitation is confined to a few malcontents . . ." Moreover, open-minded Portuguese knew that, apart from the natural impact of the Independence of India, Goans had accumulated a number of grounds for resentment against the colonial policies of Dr. Salazar. The Colonial Act, for instance, whereby the status of Goans regressed to second-class citizenship, was understandably seen as a complete betrayal of the non-discriminatory traditions of professed Portuguese colonial philosophy, especially in relation to Goa. Under this Act, inspired by a newly found concept of racial purity, natives of Portuguese overseas territories were, amongst other things, precluded from becoming Army officers. On the other hand, Dr. Salazar's argument that Goa was to be defended out of respect for the memory of "our ancestors" was a complete misrepresentation of Portuguese history, and a discredit to the ancestors themselves. Portuguese discoveries were carried out by the progressive human elements of Portugal, when European civilization had hardly emerged from feudal obscurantism. If "our ancestors" were alive today, it is quite natural that, instead of devoting any passionate interest to the diminutive enclaves of Dadra or Nagar Aveli, they would have been busy trying to solve the social problems of Portugal.

To most contemporary thinkers it seemed rational and humane that the Portuguese Government should refrain from using its political power to turn a few subservient Goans into the spokesmen of a Goan political personality—since in the long run this could only be identified with that of modern India, where 80,000 of their most able men both live and work. Not only had Portugal no major economic interest in Goa, but Dr. Salazar was aggravating his own financial problems with the military expenditure involved. At the same time, he was seriously embarrassing the Goan economy, which was virtually dependent on connections derived from its geographical position on the Indian coast, and on remittances from emigrant communities in India (in many cases the breadwinners for thousands of relatives left at home).

Even in the context and terms in which Dr. Salazar is eulogized by his admirers, his handling of the Goan issue was obviously one of the greatest blunders in the history of Portuguese foreign policy. Some Portuguese politicians realized that Mr. Nehru, widely considered to be one of the world's greatest statesmen, and the leader of a nation which could sway the destinies of mankind according to the position it would take in the world balance of power, would in consequence use his influence against Portuguese colonialism in the increasingly important Afro-Asian bloc.

Goans are the most educated of all the Portuguese colonial peoples and have taken a leading part in guiding and advising other Portuguese colonials, such as the Africans. Moreover, India has always had her own expansionist tendencies, especially in East Africa, and the role Goans could now play in the eventual emancipation of the African territories is obvious. This danger naturally invalidated both Salazar's loudly proclaimed sentimental arguments and the whispered thesis that a peaceful settlement in Goa would constitute a precedent in Portuguese colonial policy. Besides, not only were there no parallel claims at the time over any other Portuguese colonial territory, but the similar precedent set by France had had no immediate influence on her colonial policies. On the other hand, there are reasons to think that

Mr. Nehru must secretly have been pleased to have this pretext on which his United Nations Delegation could embarrass its Portuguese counterpart.

The few Portuguese who took an active stand over the issue met with very rough treatment. Dr. Salazar had meanwhile introduced constitutional changes which made it possible to have the aging Professor of Mathematics, Rui Luiz Gomes, a former Democratic candidate who had resigned in 1949 after having been publicly beaten by the State Police, arrested and held for three years for a lonely gesture of protest. The passionate mood of official hatred against Mr. Nehru personally can be judged from the fact that Igrejas Caeiro, a radio announcer, who in a rather casual way, in the course of a broadcast, referred to the Indian leader as one of the world's most brilliant statesmen, fell also into Police disgrace.

"We are fighting," said Dr. Salazar in his speech of 12th April, 1954, "so that, without offence to anyone, Goa may continue to be a memorial to Portuguese discoveries." Mass meetings, organized by the regime throughout Portugal and the Portuguese overseas territories in protest against Mr. Nehru, marked a new discovery of India— as a line of policy. The regime still lacked a valid purpose. Anti-Communist arguments were proving unconvincing: for was not Portugal herself reflected in the Government propaganda about the absence of free elections or freedom of the Press, or the presence of Police rule in the Soviet countries? And everyone knew that social achievements behind the Iron Curtain were greater than those of Dr. Salazar's Estado Novo. His exaltation at this time of the patriotic mystique of the Empire was therefore a means of promoting some measure of *unidade nacional* ("national unity"), the principle that had become the only justification for the continuance of his rule.

While it is indeed a fact that Portugal's economy would greatly suffer from the eventual disintegration of the Empire, these largely Government-promoted outbursts of feeling were also a method of diverting the attention of the Portuguese from their own real social predicament. The Past was a vehicle of escapism for the Salazar clique, and the patriotic emotions of a proud but uneducated mass were used as a major pretext for including the salvation of that clique in the process of safeguarding the "soil blessed by the blood of our ancestors". Under the pious cover and false humility of Dr. Salazar was the shrewdness of the Dictator who had learned a lot from his close connections with Nazi and Fascist techniques. He knew how to use and organize these mass meetings so as to excite national emotion in support of a mission that involved the values of the past and a determination for the future. At the same time, popularity was gained for his own ruling circle, which in its self-apotheosis, would end up by really believing itself to be both indispensable and wise.

Meanwhile, the Portuguese peasants were feeling the consequences of this false lead. They would have to join the first expeditionary forces to Goa; leave their lands and their families, and stay away in remote Asia awaiting the "enemy". Of course, the "enemy" would not come, would never come, for Mr. Nehru saw to it that human intelligence was not so disregarded as to turn the oppressed peasants of Portugal and its African dependencies, dressed up as Portuguese soldiers. into the butchers of the equally oppressed people of Goa.

CHAPTER V

THE ESTADO NOVO
AGAINST THE TIDE OF HISTORY

Fallacies of the Economic Empire

THAT THE GOA issue should mark the beginning of the diplomatic pressure by India and the Afro-Asian bloc on the wider question of the Portuguese Empire is highly symbolic in more ways than one. The Portuguese Empire in India, of which Goa, Damao and Diu are the only relics, was traditionally regarded as the crowning glory of Portugal's fifteenth-century discoveries. All Portuguese territories in Africa came under Portuguese sovereignty in the course of finding and maintaining a maritime route to India, in consequence of which the process of European imperialism in Africa and Asia began.

Centuries later, at the United Nations in New York, independent and progressive Afro-Asian states, led or influenced by India, were to become the greatest political factor in the decline and fall of the Estado Novo, as created by the heirs of the Portuguese Empire-builders. The front opened by their pressure at the United Nations, the revelation and criticism of appalling errors of omission and commission by the Portuguese colonial administration, represent more than a day of reckoning for the Empire. They have unveiled the myths behind Portuguese history.

Fighting against these myths, and often warning of the long-term consequences of their country's unrealistic obsession with the past, some Portuguese authors, much to the displeasure of official interpreters and censors, have long tried to put forward the thesis that Portugal absorbed by the "overseas idea", diverted national energies to the exploitation of its vast and dispersed Empire and neglected Portugal herself. While the capital investment necessary to the study and development of the discoveries and conquests was met from the country's resources, by the employment of cheap and forced labour, the riches reaped in India and Brazil filtered to the purses of the minority of overseas noblemen, and were squandered without leaving a trace in Portugal's social and economic development. Huge monasteries, convents and cathedrals to the glory of God, built perhaps to assuage a sense of social guilt in the benefactors, are the only landmarks of that illusory golden age of the Portuguese Empire. The sumptuous embassies to the Pope filled Portuguese imaginations instead of their stomachs. Kings disposed of the Empire as if it were personal property, often including huge areas in their daughters' dowries, or in settlement of disputes with other powers, undeterred by the claim of colonial philosophers that Portuguese possessions were Provinces of a single nation.

Portugal came to resemble some of its ruined noblemen. Impotent to adapt itself to evolution and reality, it deluded itself that the past achievements of Portuguese expansionism would act as a deterrent to the ambitions of new imperialists. The constant threats to its Empire further absorbed and wasted national attention. Instead of facing the problems of its own economy, the nation engaged in pathetic protests against international injustice, and went to church to pray for the salvation of huge and empty areas in Africa, as if God was likely to discriminate between old and new imperialist causes. Every time an economic component such as India, and later Brazil, faded away, Portugal was faced with serious problems arising from the stagnant condition of its own economy and the stratification of its society. Cut off from the industrial revolution, the Portuguese economy was a hostage to circumstance. Political power was concentrated in the hands of a minority of landlords and nabobs who had no such problems as the creation of a market for industrial goods or raising the standard of living. On the contrary, Portuguese poverty was a guarantee of the plentiful supply of cheap labour.

Portugal is still the owner of one of the largest colonial Empires in the world. What is left of the Empire is by no means inconsiderable. Portuguese territories cover an area of over 800,000 square miles, or roughly that of the whole of Western Europe. Two of them, Angola and Mozambique, although largely undeveloped, are economic factors which in some way or another touch the Portuguese economy at nearly every point. Yet, even so, Portugal's national income remains one of the lowest in Europe. The following table, which compares the revenue of Portugal with that of a group of non-colonialist European nations of smaller population, is a sure indication that the myth of the Empire having contributed to the aggrandisement of Portugal is hardly consistent with social and economic fact:

		1957 Population in millions	1957 National income (milliards of U.S. dollars)	Approx. income *per capita* (dollars)
Sweden ..	..	7·4	9·3	1,250
Switzerland	..	5·2	6·4	1,230
Denmark	..	4·5	3·9	865
Austria ..	..	7·0	3·8	545
Norway	..	3·5	3·2	820
Greece ..	..	8·2	2·4	290
Portugal	..	9·0	1·8	200

Since Dr. Salazar came to power to prevent any tampering with "sacred" principles, the Estado Novo's economic policies have aimed exclusively at raising the standard of living by means of an increase in production, instead of adopting agrarian or fiscal reforms which would compromise the structure of Portuguese society. If, therefore, Dr. Salazar's first task was the administration of the budget, his second was to lay down the basis of a neo-imperialist economic policy, which would increase national wealth by effective exploitation of the Portuguese Empire, especially in Angola and Mozambique. The economy was largely dependent on the export of a handful of commodities, such as cork, canned fish and wines, and a variety of other agricultural and mineral products on a smaller scale, in exchange for industrial raw materials and fuels, machinery, vehicles and those manufactured goods necessary for the social and economic upkeep of the country. The expansion of the Portuguese economy had therefore to be adapted to collaboration with that of the colonial territories.

At the inaugural session of the Economic Conference of the Portuguese Colonial Empire, held in Lisbon in June 1936 to study the foundations of the neo-imperial economy, Dr. Salazar delivered a speech in which he analysed the demographic situation in Portugal and stated that more than one million people had emigrated in the previous fifty years alone. The annual increase of population was then eighty thousand people, but it would soon reach one hundred thousand, which meant that, if "no untoward circumstances arise, especially if the

Portuguese are not converted to the practice of birth control as advocated by pretended modern civilization, and even if preference in Brazil for the Portuguese emigrant should continue, Portugal will have to support and maintain, within thirty years from now, a population of from nine to ten million." In 1864 there were 45.5 inhabitants per square kilometre; in 1890 there were 55; and in 1930 there were just over 74. In the Oporto district the average was 335, Lisbon 330, Funchal 260 and in Braga 152. "When we reach the [national] figure of nine million we shall have in Portugal and the adjacent islands a hundred inhabitants per square kilometre, and unless new outlets of activity can be found the Mother Country will not be able to support this figure, except at a progressively lower standard of living."

According to calculations made by the Ministry of Works at the time, it was estimated that only 150,000 hectares would be capable of reclamation by irrigation, moreover the first stage of the work would take years to complete and would cost some £6 million. Even if it were possible to utilize all the land that could be irrigated, this would only allow for the establishment of 150,000 families.

"Uncultivated parts of the country are rare," stated Dr. Salazar, "and in the Alemtejo there are none at all. Generally speaking it can be said that we have utilized all the available land with the exception of those barren tracts which could be made valuable by irrigation, and the dunes and hills which have not yet been afforested."

The solution would either have to be found through emigration to the colonies, or by the more active development of the industries of the country. Through the latter alternative the demographic surplus could be absorbed, and it would be possible for dense populations to exist without discomfort; but in this case it would be necessary to establish favourable conditions for industrial development, and the expansion of industry in Portugal was faced with such basic problems as lack of capital, technical deficiencies, the cost of fuel and electric power and the need for raw materials and markets—i.e., practically every element was missing except cheap labour. "In the circumstances," concluded Dr. Salazar, "the logical solution is for the colonies to produce the raw material and to sell it to the Mother Country in exchange for manufactured goods."

The "One Nation" Economy

In order to pursue an ambitious economic reconstruction programme, which would imply complete economic interdependence between Portugal and its overseas territories, the colonial policies of Dr. Salazar's regime aimed at perpetuating Portuguese sovereignty by giving constitutional force to the theory of a *nação una* ("one nation") which had been advanced by several Portuguese colonialists. The late General Norton de Matos, one of the leading authorities on Portuguese Africa and a former Governor of Angola, explained this principle in his books, *A Nação Una* and others, where he analysed the traditional Portuguese colonial policies, held in common with the Spaniards, who likewise regarded their Latin American colonies as Provinces. He claimed that ever since, many centuries ago, the Portuguese people had first met with men of other colours, religions, habits and customs, it had been their Christian resolution not only to evangelize, but to construct out of the various communities a great nation bound together in complete unity. Such theories attempted to solve the economic and political dilemma of diverting national capital and manpower to the Empire, only to face the eventuality of emancipation, and consequent dislocation of the Portuguese economy; but General Norton de Matos can be said to have stood for a kind of Portuguese version of the British Commonwealth idea. He was himself a bitter opponent of the Salazar regime, was at one time an exponent of Angolan autonomy and was a Democratic candidate in 1949.

The four principles governing the policy of the Estado Novo towards the overseas Provinces are largely based on traditional colonial philosophies such as he described, but when taken into the nationalistic mystique they became distorted to the advantage of the central government. Essentially these principles aim at: (*a*) political unity, (*b*) spiritual assimilation, (*c*) administrative differentiation, and (*d*) economic solidarity. Political unity, in theory, would mean equal rights for all the Provinces, without priorities for Metropolitan interests. While the overseas territories would be subject to the same central government in Lisbon, and be represented at the National Assembly, administrative differentiation would be pursued as a deliberate policy in order to resolve more efficiently all purely regional and local problems. Colonial populations would become citizens of Portugal should they assimilate Portuguese culture. These first three principles form a necessary political and legislative background for the fourth— the policy of "economic solidarity". This, however, is in practice no more than a euphemism for economic subjection, since, under Dr.

Salazar's regime, the Central Government in Lisbon has seen to it that all colonial development should in some way or other be subordinated to Metropolitan interests.

The economic framework of the Corporative State, with all its authoritarian and bureaucratic implications, has been extended to Portuguese Africa. In addition to preferential customs tariffs (in some cases fifty per cent below those prevailing for foreign goods), stiff protective import restrictions were introduced. Special Economic Co-ordination Boards were set up, and their function, although their expenses are met from the budgets of the colonies themselves, is to control import and export trade in the interests of Metropolitan Portugal. Economically speaking, the "nationalism" of the "one nation" is really *metropolitanism*. Although the pattern of Portugal's economic relationships with its overseas territories is essentially similar to that of other colonial systems, in this case it implies that the African territories obtain little that is useful to them, and have to contend with a number of problems arising from Portugal's own social and economic underdevelopment.

Since the consumer market in Portuguese Africa consists mainly of some six million Africans in Mozambique and another four and a half million Africans in Angola with a remarkably low purchasing power, the consumption of available and suitable Portuguese produce, such as wine, had to be stimulated amongst them by means which included an administrative prohibition on the making of native beverages (under the pretext that the popular "Lisbon water" was less physically harmful). On the other hand, since Portugal had neither secondary industry nor enough capital and technology to survey, and possibly exploit, mineral raw materials in its African territories, Portuguese industrial development was conditioned to the supply of cheap agricultural raw materials and foodstuffs. For instance, a system of forced cotton growing was introduced in Mozambique and Angola.

Imported from Africa after an elementary ginning process, colonial cotton, or "white gold", has fostered the development of the important textile industry in Portugal. The finished product, in the form of cheap fancy cloth, is exported back to the African markets. The exchange of the raw cotton for cotton textiles not only pays, to a large extent, in terms of currency, for the import of the raw material, but leaves a substantial margin for Portugal's own requirements, and for export to foreign countries. Sugar, vegetable oils and other tropical and sub-tropical products are imported in a semi-processed state and either consumed in Portugal or re-exported abroad. Prices, fixed by the Government's Co-ordinating Boards, are in most cases considerably below world levels.

Currently, an average of some twelve and a half per cent of Portuguese imports come from Angola and Mozambique, while these countries buy over twenty-five per cent of Portuguese exports. The relative importance of cotton and wine in the balance of trade between Portugal and the Portuguese overseas territories can be assessed in the following figures:

Portugal's imports CIF 1959–1960			Portugal's exports FOB 1959–1960		
	Millions of pounds			Millions of pounds	
Total including other items	24·0	28·0	Total including other items	30·0	30·0
Sugar	4·9	5·3	Wines	2·7	3·9
Cotton, raw	7·6	10·7	Cotton cloth & manufactures	6·4	5·6
Coffee	2·2	1·9	Leather footwear	0·8	0·7
Sisal	1·3	1·7	Tyres	0·9	1·6

The influence of Mozambique and Angola in the Portuguese economy is well reflected in the balance of payments. Portuguese exports pay for less than half of the imports, and in 1959 Portugal's deficit in its balance of trade with the world was over £53 million. The country's only major source of invisible earnings is tourism, from which the surplus revenue, at an annual rate of some £5·2 million, was much the same in 1959 as the deficit on the transport balance. Yet the overall balance of payments in the Escudo Area shows a consistent annual surplus of some £16 million. The gold and foreign exchange reserves of the Bank of Portugal stood at £298 million at the end of 1959, a reserve which accounts for the respectability of the escudo.

Portugal's economic development under Dr. Salazar's Estado Novo owes much to invisible earnings from colonial sources, and the expression "strong escudo" would better have been coined "colonial escudo"—for the colonial escudos filter into Portuguese economy in the form of profits from Metropolitan-owned enterprises, which include the bulk of the productive and banking interests, and the shipping businesses which handle financial and traffic operations to and from Portugal. Money remittances from emigrants, the payment of retirement pensions to former colonial public servants residing in Portugal, the fares on Portuguese-protected shipping-lines and airways, as well as the savings spent in Portugal by tourists from Africa are by no means an inconsiderable source of revenue. The overseas territories ultimately meet these debts from their own foreign currency and gold, for lack of Metropolitan escudos, which they only obtain in moderate quantity in the course of their "economic-solidarity" connections with Portugal. Control of Foreign Exchange is centralized in the Bank of Portugal, Lisbon.

"Dictatorship does not pay"

The duration of Dr. Salazar's regime in Portugal invalidates the analysis of Portuguese economic development on a purely domestic basis. For one thing, the short-lived and troubled Republican Governments inherited a bankrupt economy which was greatly affected by the First World War. Under the Estado Novo, on the contrary, the country benefited, as has been seen, from war conditions, because of its position of friendly business neutrality with all sides, and especially from the export of strategic raw minerals, such as wolfram, to Germany. Economic comparisons with foreign countries are equally involved, and often misleading. Portugal's natural resources are amongst the poorest in Europe, yet most European countries of roughly comparable population and geographical and economic scale had to face tremendous post-war reconstruction problems, and are, none the less, not only currently enjoying a much higher standard of living, but showing a higher rate of economic development.

Although Portugal has no political or cultural relations with the Soviet countries, China and India, which together account for half the world's population, the country cannot be maintained, for many obvious reasons, as an "island of separateness", in complete isolation from the outside world. It is because of the necessity of bowing in some measure to the wind of post-war internationalism and seeking membership of NATO and UN that Dr. Salazar has laid himself open to world criticism and his quarrel with the influential Indian group was so untimely. Politically, the regime has tried to relax some of its most evident dictatorial features. (Children no longer have to shout three times that it is Dr. Salazar who commands; Dr. Salazar no longer has Mussolini's autographed photograph conspicuously displayed on his desk; the right of "habeas corpus" has been publicly introduced, although its observance is privately conditioned to the Government's convenience; the Portuguese colonies have been renamed Provinces.) Economically, comparison with other NATO countries has exposed Portugal's shortcomings.

Portugal joined NATO in 1949, and thus became a defender of civic freedoms its citizens themselves do not enjoy. With diplomatic protection from Great Britain and the United States, and the speculative sanction of the Soviet bloc itself, which was interested in bargaining the admission of some remote Asian republics, Portugal became a member of the United Nations and its subsidiaries, such as UNESCO, while the basic Declaration of the Rights of Man, to which the Estado Novo subscribed, is denied in the letter and spirit of her laws—and above all in their application. Membership of assorted scientific, social and labour organizations is enjoyed in spite of the fact that labour legislation and practice in both Portugal and its overseas territories reduce workers to a state of serfdom. In its political and diplomatic connections, the Portuguese rulers have benefited, until recently, from the international principle of non-intervention in domestic policies. This modern nicety is also unmistakably contradicted in many ways in various parts of the world, and in Portugal it is specifically negated and disguised under economic and military aid, which is ultimately used to maintain the oppression of defenceless populations both in Metropolitan Portugal and its Empire.

In the field of economic relationships, however, Dr. Salazar is faced with some embarrassing problems. Portugal's inevitable adherence to the European Free Trade Association is a good illustration of the new demands and responsibilities of her role in the international field. The fact that Portugal has the lowest income per head, the highest tariff barriers and is the least advanced of all the Seven members of the Association has created a number of difficulties. Portuguese ministers who, in some cases, are directly interested as landlords and business men in the Portuguese export trade, have personal reasons to be worried by economic divisions such as the Six and the Seven. Portugal's ten main exports, which account for sixty-seven per cent of Portuguese trade, formerly went indiscriminately to the Six (thirty-seven per cent in 1959) and to the Seven (twenty-six per cent), and any market restrictions or dislocation of trade can only add to the problems that arise from the almost total reliance of Portuguese trade on a small variety of products, some of which are dependent on climatic conditions, not only in Portugal but in remote Africa. Furthermore, Portuguese industrial exports, the bulk again consisting of a small variety of commodities, such as cotton textiles, processed fish and timber products, are precisely in the category that meets with high competition.

Powerless to arrest the foreign politicians responsible for such upsetting innovations, planners in the Estado Novo are currently engaged in a race for progress. Since the adjustment of the Portuguese economy to international trends implies the need to raise the purchasing power of the Portuguese market, it will not even be surprising if, in the process, some social development is achieved in Portugal. But there is a formidable amount of ground to make up.

Since the Corporative State likes to regard itself as the type of dictatorship that specializes in fast economic development, one would expect, after thirty-three years, to find the annual rate of expansion considerably greater than that of democratic regimes, if for no other reason than to justify the intolerable suspension of civil liberties. Admittedly Dr. Salazar's regime has only in recent years found the financial resources with which to meet the costs of its Six Year Development Plans (1953–58 and 1959–64), covering agricultural, afforestation and land-settlement schemes, the production of hydro-electric power, the establishment of basic secondary industries and the expansion and/or improvement of the network of communications and transport, and the combined programme has not yet had its full effect on the country's economy; but it is almost incredible that, in all this time, things should have advanced so little. To start with, at 4.4 per cent, the Portuguese rate of economic growth is still lower than that of such East European countries as Hungary, Czechoslovakia and Bulgaria. Austria and West Germany have reached a rate of 7.7 per cent and Italy 5.4 per cent, all three having reverted from a totalitarian to a democratic system of government.

In an analysis of the problems of economic expansion in Portugal, Professors Pereira de Moura and Teixeira Pinto state (*Problemas do Crescimento Economico Portugues*, 1958):

Post-war gross national production rose at an annual rate of four per cent, which is equivalent to an annual rate *per capita* of some three per cent. This increase reflects a reasonable development, but we should bear in mind that other countries have had a more considerable development . . . In the same period the group of countries belonging to the OEEC had an average annual rate of gross increase of six per cent, equivalent to a *per capita* rate of five per cent . . . If we wanted to forecast our future position we should . . . conclude that it would take eighty years for us to reach the *present* American gross rate of production *per capita* or forty years to reach the *present* rate of the OEEC countries. If we increase our rate of growth to five per cent we shall be able to reach the *present* average annual rate of gross production in Western European countries in 1980.

With the situation expressed in such bald terms, no one can be surprised if there is a growing movement, inside the country and out, towards a complete reassessment of the historical myths that hold Portugal and its Empire together.

CHAPTER VI

THE OPPOSITION AND THE NEW OPPOSITION

The Constitutional Coup d'État

UNDER THE ESTADO NOVO, national unity may not have been achieved but national uniformity surely has. Censorship and police rules have left the Portuguese people inarticulate and reduced the various territories that are supposed to be Provinces of the same nation to political isolation. There is hardly any economic or social communication between them. Today, as in the days before the Estado Novo, "Portuguese politics" has a different meaning for different people, depending on who they are and where they are; and if there is any common ground between them it is a widespread emotional phenomenon, a spontaneous resistance to oppressive rule.

The majority of Portuguese intellectuals and professionally responsible men, who form the core of the officially non-existent "opposition", find the sophisms and paradoxes of the Estado Novo so transparent and so offensive to intelligence that they prefer a self-imposed exile in their own country to any form of collaboration with the regime. Most expressions of non-conformism are to be found in Portuguese literature, although literary fiction is also subject to repressive measures, including outright suppression. Professors, lecturers, poets, writers, artists, journalists, forming groups such as that around the magazine *Seara Nova*, have been the favourite target of the Portuguese Security Police and some have sought exile abroad. Yet the hypocrisy of the regime extends to the point of having held an exhibition commemorating its thirtieth anniversary in which suppressed newspapers and periodicals, and books whose authors had been persecuted by the police, were displayed in spite of the protests of the writers concerned.

In a country where the Press has to be *Visada pela Censura* (Approved by the Censor) every paradox is possible: repressive censorship and police rules which are explained as a means of defending the freedom of Portuguese people and the Christian way of life: an economy based on the Corporative principles of controlled free enterprise, but of which the foundation stone is the labour of compulsory volunteer workers; a foreign policy opposed simultaneously to the Soviet Bloc and the Western powers. It is therefore not surprising that—according to the definition currently accepted by the regime's own leaders—the only way an officially non-existent opposition could possibly overthrow Dr. Salazar peacefully would be by means of a "constitutional *coup d'état*".

The constitutional *coup d'état* can be summed up as follows: the President of the Republic could, if he dared to use the powers conferred on him by the Constitution, dismiss the Prime Minister, Dr. Salazar. With the appointment of a new Prime Minister, and a new cabinet, the way would be open for sweeping legal change. Since the President was until recently supposed to be elected every seven years by direct universal suffrage it follows that it was theoretically possible for the regime's opponents, improvised into Candidacy Committees, to try to have a President of their own choice elected. Should the elections be free, any new cabinet could turn the Government machine against the Estado Novo men themselves without the immediate necessity of even effecting any major legal reform. In such circumstances it is unlikely that they would resist the temptation to let those people have a taste of their own laws, including provisions for the detention of any citizen for lengthy periods on vaguely defined security charges. As some of the State Police are most professionally minded men, it would also be possible to whisper the same sort of instructions as have often resulted in the physical and mental ruin of some of the regime's opponents.

In fact, however, the periodic election of a President has merely provided the regime with an extremely good opportunity to bring its police records up to date. By means of allowing a rationed thirty days of freedom, during which censorship was relaxed, a number of otherwise quiet citizens would come into the open, either as members of Candidacy Committees, guest speakers or electoral campaign hands. The first constitutional *coup d'état* attempted under the Estado Novo came in the form of Presidential elections in 1949. The old and highly respected General Norton de Matos was the opposition candidate. He was promptly proclaimed by the Government propaganda machine to be an unwitting puppet of the Communists or, alternatively, a dangerous freemason. One of the ethical highlights of this electoral period was the use made by the Government campaigners of a phrase of the General to the effect that "before the last moment of Dr. Salazar's public life" he would demand an apology from him for a statement de Matos had regarded as offensive. This was taken as a threat to Dr. Salazar's life, and the Government Press denounced his whole campaign as murderous. Carried away, a Government supporter shouted that "in the event of electoral danger" the Spaniards would help, "as we helped them during the Spanish Civil War". The Army and Air Force engaged in large-scale exercises up and down the country. There were no guarantees as to the fairness of the elections and, after vainly appealing to the Estado Novo's acting President, Marshal Carmona, who was then seeking re-election, to do the same, General Norton de Matos resigned on the eve of the poll. The Government's candidate having been duly renominated, conditions reverted to the usual pattern. For some time, under the cloak of silence provided by censorship, all those law-abiding citizens who had come forward in support of General Norton de Matos were "investigated", or became unknowing "lighthouses" for the Police as they circulated amongst their friends.

The second attempt at a change of government came in 1951, on the death of President Carmona, who had of late been complaining to his intimate friends and visitors that "he felt like a bird in a golden cage". The golden cage was the Presidential palace. This time there were two opposition candidates, Professor Rui Luiz Gomes, for the Democrats, and Admiral Quintao Meireles, for the Independents. The Democrats were immediately accused of having insulted the Blessed Virgin merely because someone had commented on the political significance and timing of the apparition at Fatima, now turned into the greatest religious resort in Portugal. Professor Rui Luiz Gomes, a Presidential candidate and well known as a mathematician, was physically assaulted by the Security Police, together with some of his supporters, at an electoral meeting not far from Lisbon. Admiral Quintao Meireles, a devout Catholic, never fully recovered from the personal humiliations to which he was subjected. Finding human excrement on the door bell of his own residence he threatened to hand over to the Government all his medals and decorations. Following the example of General Norton de Matos, he resigned on the eve of election day, with a farewell Manifesto to the nation in which he described the Government's lack of civility.

One of the prominent supporters of Admiral Quintao Meireles was Captain Henrique Galvao, formerly a close friend of Dr. Salazar, a director of the National Broadcasting Services and at one time Governor of the District of Huila, Angola. A man of great charm and versatility, he is also a well-known playwright; in love with life, as a whole, he is a man who enjoys Shakespeare and opera as much as the excitement of big game hunting in Africa. He had fallen into disgrace for having dared to take his job as Senior Colonial Inspector seriously. In a number of successive reports about conditions in Angola he had exposed some of the alarming features of Portuguese colonialism. After the elections, he busied himself trying to form an opposition group called the Portuguese Civic Organization. When its offices were raided Henrique Galvao was arrested, together with other people who were attending a meeting.

On December 9th, 1952, charged with plotting an anti-constitutional *coup d'état*, Henrique Galvao was sentenced to a preliminary three years in prison. For the next seven years he was kept in jail on a series of charges. He was indeed one of the main anti-Estado Novo conspirators and managed to publish several pamphlets and revolutionary poems which were printed and smuggled out of prison by some of the prison officers themselves. Among his fellow conspirators were certain prominent Army officers, some of whom, having had better proposi- tions, are now more senior than ever, either in the Portuguese Army or in the plutocratic hierarchy. An exception was one of his most faithful friends, General Humberto Delgado, then Portugal's Air Attaché in Washington and NATO representative. He frequently visited Galvao in prison and they often commented that, after all, from the point of view of political activity, there was really little difference between being in jail and being apparently free in the sunny and orderly concentration camp that Portugal is for Dr. Salazar's opponents.

Indeed, political life went on as usual. The Government's opponents, too involved socially and financially to have much choice between exile abroad or exile in Portugal itself, mostly remained as inmates, while the concentration camp guards, in the guise of casual patrons of pavement cafés, domestic servants, artisans or office colleagues, kept an eye on them. Journalists, from sheer habit, went on writing for the censorship in such a vein that the censors themselves wondered whether they were still necessary at all; the security police went on with their routine investigations, often for no other reason than to justify their salaries; the Government secretariat went on contrasting the fraternal goodwill existing between Portugal and Portuguese Africa with the agitation prevailing in most other parts of the world, as if Portugal's peace were not merely that of any occupied country. It seemed that Dr. Salazar might have succeeded in turning the Portuguese into one of "those happy peoples who do not have to think".

The New Generation in Revolt

At a time when the regime was beginning to feel the first effects of a degree of saturation and division, centred around its own secret issues of right versus left, liberal versus traditionalist, Republican versus Monarchist, and even the Army was divided over the person of that strongman's strong man, the Monarchist Defence Minister, Lieutenant-Colonel Santos Costa, came the June 1958 elections. The Estado Novo had greater need than ever to appear democratic, because of the increasing number of its international connections with the Western countries. As it was not even a democracy for the insiders (National Union followers did not vote or decide their own leadership, and had to accept a good measure of autocratic control), there was an increasing number of dissidents. At the same time, a new generation of men, who since their infancy had been quietly watching the ethics, methods and character of the regime, had now reached maturity. For this generation the Republican issue was invalid, since the Estado Novo men, including Dr. Salazar himself, had had more to do with the Republican period than any of the young Portuguese. For them it appeared that, even if the negative aspects of the "Republican" period had to be accepted, the Estado Novo was just a "Republican" faction that had overcome all the weaker factions. Furthermore, there was hardly any indication as to the term of the Estado Novo's mission, which had already had thirty-two years in which to complete the political re-education of the country—towards, one would presume, the restitution of civil liberties.

To everybody's surprise, Dr. Salazar had General Craveiro Lopes, then President, replaced as a Candidate by Admiral Americo Tomas. It seems that President Craveiro Lopes had fallen into the bad graces of the all-powerful Minister of Defence, Lieutenant-Colonel Santos

Costa, and that, in spite of his status as President, he was now the losing party.

The improvised association of individuals known as the "Opposition" was itself divided. The old, traditional, democratic opposition, comprising the left and socialist, including Communist, factions, soon entered the ring and finally settled for the introduction of Mr. Arlindo Vicente, a barrister, as their Democratic Candidate. Meanwhile a vast group of liberals, dissidents as well as democrats, mainly concentrated at Oporto, decided that General Humberto Delgado should be the Independent Candidate. His platform offered, essentially, a breathing space between his election (which would spell the end of the Estado Novo) and a Democratic form of Government.

Largely owing to General Delgado's modern outlook and dynamism, and to the spirit of his campaign slogans ("We are tired of being treated as a flock of sheep" and "Fear is ended"), Portugal was shaken into a sudden awakening. Mass enthusiasm was unparalleled in Portuguese history. Over three hundred thousand people turned out to acclaim him, while, throughout Portugal, crowds shouted "save us!" and women and children kissed his hands in the surge of emotion.

At a meeting near Lisbon it was agreed that Mr. Arlindo Vicente should resign his candidacy, while the opposition would join forces in an all out effort against the Estado Novo. As election day came nearer the Government revealed the extent of its panic. Lieutenant-Colonel Santos Costa publicly declared that the armed forces would support the National Union Candidate. The Police killed a number of unarmed civilians in Lisbon. The acting President was urged by his own family, his liberal sons and his brave wife, to intervene and postpone the elections, and the conflict between the President and the Defence Minister became a serious problem. In point of fact, President Craveiro Lopes is known to have been imprisoned in his own palace to preclude him from effecting a military coup known to have been planned to take place at the beginning of June, a few days before election day.

While these events were kept from public knowledge, other incidents in connection with the elections revealed to even the most comformist and apolitical citizen the true face of the Estado Novo. People carrying Delgado's voting cards for distribution were arrested; in Madeira the customs required some sort of certificate of origin for its consignment of opposition ballot cards, while the official candidate was dispensed from this formality in respect of his. In

Portuguese Africa the worry was that these cards, one or other of which must be used for the actual vote according to the choice of candidate, would turn out to be in conspicuously different colours. On the day of the elections the country faced moral collapse.

The Opposition could not count the votes. They were counted by the Government's own trusted "nationalists", behind tables placed in the darker corners of polling-stations. But, apart from the Government's own admission that General Delgado had obtained some twenty five per cent of the total votes, the Portuguese people could judge the results for themselves, from the extraordinary electoral tactics of the Government. These ranged from giving Government voting cards in sealed envelopes to country people—so that, while using free Government transport to the polls, they should not change the vote on the way—to allowing multiple voting, under a fixed rate, even on behalf of long-deceased voters. In Portuguese Africa, where there are some inland stations with no more than a handful of voters, absentees gasped to find that the Government candidate in their home area had somehow claimed a one hundred per cent poll. While the votes were being counted in one Lourenço Marques area the lights went out suddenly, but candles were promptly produced.

Portugal has never been quite the same since then. Soon after the election a letter signed by the Bishop of Oporto and addressed to Dr. Salazar was circulated and reproduced throughout the country. In this letter the Bishop of Oporto declared that the Government's policies could not be reconciled with the principles of Catholic sociology, and that the Corporative labour laws had aimed at "depriving labourers of their natural rights of association". Other prominent Catholics, including the leaders of Catholic organizations, were promoting the clandestine publication of manifestoes and memoranda to the Government. Most Opposition activities were centred around General Delgado's post-electoral protests. However, police repression was also being renewed. The open discussion of the country's problems in the month preceding the elections was once again providing a list of names to bring the police files up to date. Arrests were being made throughout Portugal, Angola and Mozambique. For the simple "crime" of inviting the late Aneurin Bevan to come to Portugal and lecture on non-Portuguese political subjects, the Government arrested four well-known Portuguese intellectuals, the youngest being a septuagenarian. In official notes published in the Press, the Government further announced that legal proceedings against General Delgado were on the way.

The trend of events then took a dramatic turn. General Delgado was warned through a reliable source connected with the Security Police that there was a plan to arrest him after a framed popular manifestation which would be turned into a riot with Police provocation. He decided to take refuge at the Brazilian Embassy in Lisbon.

The Brazilian Ambassador was then Mr. Alvaro Lins, one of the most prominent writers in the Portuguese language and a well-known democrat. During the term of his diplomatic mission to Portugal he had quietly been judging for himself the nature of Portuguese politics. A man of great sensitivity and a modern mind, he could not help being moved by the saga of the Portuguese people. To him General Delgado's predicament appeared as the epitome of the whole Portuguese situation and he promptly granted him asylum. This provided Mr. Lins with a unique opportunity to confirm his impressions.

The unsophisticated General Delgado, who reacts to the Estado Novo's political philosophies with healthy peasant laughter, had known all along that the only way to overthrow Dr. Salazar's regime was an *anti*-constitutional *coup d'état*. On the 17th July, 1958, since General Craveiro Lopes (the acting President who had been replaced as the *Uniao Nacional*'s nominee by Admiral Tomas) had badly bungled his attempt to remove Dr. Salazar as far away from Portugal as possible by force, Delgado wrote a passionate letter to four Portuguese Army chiefs, inviting them to open rebellion. The letter was addressed to Generals Botelho Moniz (Chief of General Staff, Defence), Frederico Lopes da Silva (President of the Supreme Military Court), Costa Macedo (Chief of the Air Force General Staff) and Beleza Ferraz (Chief of the Army General Staff). It claimed that the elections had been rigged (a fact that was surely not news to them) and that a pre-requisite of Dr. Salazar's removal was the summary dismissal of Lieutenant-Colonel Santos Costa, the Minister of Defence, who had all along been manipulating the armed services at a high-ranking level so that trusted Monarchist officers should always be handy. It went on to point out that Dr. Salazar, who had recently told a foreign journalist that he was the father of the Portuguese, "a father who listens to his sons, but decides on their behalf", was treating his "children" very badly indeed. According to his letter—supported by the statements of hundreds of Portuguese—a horrifying list of "investigation" methods was being used by the police, including: "extraction of teeth, the twisting of genital organs until the victim faints, the breaking of jaws, and assorted brutalities, such as forcing men to stand up for days and nights on end and kicking them until they dragged themselves up again". Furthermore, Decree no. 40,550 of March 12th, 1956, had given the Security Police powers to jail men indefinitely at will. After recalling the historic example of the Nazi generals who attempted to overthrow Hitler, General Delgado, in conclusion, appealed to the pride of the Army with a warning that a civilian struggle might well break out before they had acted: "It is necessary that we should organize an adequate concentration of troops, or at least an alert, so that they may be ready to enter into combat with Lieutenant-Colonel Costa's forces should these fail to understand that the hour of National Liberation had arrived ... Needless to say, I am at your disposal for the study and execution of this plan, and I am ready to go with those who may want to follow me ... I do not want to end without stating that I am seriously worried by the popular feeling that prevails against the Government, especially against the two tyrants [Dr. Salazar and Lieutenant-Colonel Santos Costa]".

The Portuguese Government turned General Delgado's political asylum into a tragi-comedy. They claimed that he was free to leave— but on 3rd February, 1959, the situation around the Brazilian Embassy was thus described by the Ambassador himself in his diary: "The Embassy continues surrounded by policemen. Why? Nobody knows. How *conspicuous* the *secret* PIDE men are! They all have the same kind of uniform which betrays them upon sight: the same overcoat in summer and winter, the back deformed by the heavy shape of firearms, which such men always wear upon their hips, hat brims pulled over one eye, as in the best tradition of the cinema—except that these are real-life gangsters ..."[1]

Perhaps because police attention and personnel were diverted to the Brazilian Embassy, Henrique Galvao meanwhile managed to escape from a hospital where he was being kept under permanent guard. After going into hiding for a few days, he turned up at the Argentinian Embassy disguised as a delivery-man and applied for political asylum as well.

An attempted *coup d'état* involving both General Delgado and Captain Galvao was aborted on the 19th March, 1959. Emphasizing the

[1] Alvaro Lins, *op. cit.*, p. 217.

hardening mood of events, even Father Perestrelo, who had acted as host to the conspirators in his Church, was arrested carrying guns under his cassock. Latin American Embassies in Lisbon were kept busy giving asylum to scores of "opposition" leaders, while others were escaping into exile abroad.

The Army, displaying symptoms of the general instability, forced a major Government reorganization. An unexplained change of the Cabinet brought the replacement of unpopular Lieutenant-Colonel Santos Costa, a Monarchist, by General Botelho Moniz, a Republican. In a further attempt to control the situation, the Government hastily amended the constitution, abolishing once and for all the possibility of a "constitutional *coup d'état*". The election of the President was transferred from the realm of universal suffrage to an electoral college, comprised of members of the National Assembly and the Corporative Chamber—where, of course, all the existing ruling clique is represented.

Then followed the reunion of General Delgado, Captain Galvao and other anti-Salazar leaders in Latin America and the reorganization of Portuguese "opposition" abroad. The *Movimento Nacional Independente* easily found thousands of supporters amongst the large Portuguese communities scattered throughout Latin American countries, especially in Brazil, and its network of activities throughout the world came to include the publication of periodicals, broadcasts through sympathetic foreign stations in Africa and official representation in London and Paris.

Although liaison with "opposition" elements remaining in Portugal is made difficult by the Government's virtual control over communications (including correspondence), free Portuguese are still in close touch with the situation there. Widespread political neurosis continues. The Government followers see Communists everywhere; the opponents of the regime are over suspicious, and often find themselves policing even hypothetical police agents. Government supporters engage in printing pseudo-opposition pamphlets denouncing some of the opposition's most dedicated underground fighters as informers, and an appalling confusion is thereby created.

Under censorship, the Portuguese are completely at the mercy of Police rule. In 1960 alone there were 3,811 trials leading to convictions for crimes against religion, the security of the State and other political offences. The situation has been most vividly expressed in a letter addressed to Dr. Salazar in February 1960 by the former Presidential candidate, Arlindo Vicente, in which he described a brutal police raid on a peaceful gathering of men and women, old people and children, who were paying homage to those who had died for Republican ideals at the Prado do Repouso cemetery in Oporto. The raid, carried out under cover of censorship, coincided with a much-publicized banquet commemorating the civil war against the Republic, and the writer of the letter felt himself to have been singled out for special attention by the police. He recalled a time in 1920 when certain pamphlets were being circulated at Coimbra University, setting out the defence of three professors (of whom Dr. Salazar was one) before an official enquiry, in which they had been accused of offending against the ideas and political system then in force. He pointed out that he had been deeply impressed at the time, not only by the stand the professors had made for their rights, but by the fact that the Government of the day had accepted their arguments and praised their defence of the rights of all men.

Today no one, not even Dr. Salazar himself, can know exactly what the dominant currents of public opinion are. Men mounted on tigers, those who support the regime, are too afraid to climb off. Since, for them, Dr. Salazar has become the synonym of authority, no one, not even the President, who has powers to dismiss the Government, dares to challenge the unknown potentialities of the political situation. The country has been led to the point where the state of health of a single man, seventy-three years old, is still the best gauge of the state of Portuguese politics. When one considers that the destiny and freedom of some twenty-two million people in Portugal and its Empire depend on Portuguese politics, one is no longer surprised that at the end of January, 1961, the *Movimento Nacional Independente*, represented by Captain Henrique Galvao, took drastic action. The gun-point seizure by stow away rebels of the Portuguese luxury liner, *Santa Maria*, far away in the Caribbean, made Portugal's cry for freedom heard in the four corners of the earth.

Santa Maria!

After seizing control of the *Santa Maria*, the first thing Henrique Galvao did was to play Tchaikovsky's "1812" overture, as if he dreamed his country was already freed of the oppressor; but, alas, there is no way in modern times to defeat tyrants quickly, to take a

Bastille by storm or to impose a Magna Carta simply by arresting a king. The fight for freedom must always inspire novel adventures adapted to the times.

Never was there an act of piracy more politically justified than the *coup* of the *Santa Maria*. Its engineers were determined to make the best of their flamboyant action to compel world attention for their cause. It was the only blow that could momentarily numb Dr. Salazar and his bodyguard. Inside Portugal, under the cloak of censorship, when anything "subversive" is suspected the first people to be arrested are the treasurers and contributors. There have been people who have been arrested for giving sixpence to an embryonic political party. Unlike African liberation movements, which have the open support of the Afro-Asian and Soviet blocs, Portuguese democrats have to apply all the traditional talent of their people for the manipulation of meagre budgets to their revolutionary investment. Deprived of financial means, Portuguese political activity is limited in general to the cheap verbal transmission of news. "Political action" is mostly confined to the translation of reports and news stories from the foreign Press, such as *The Guardian*, the *Observer*, the *New Statesman*, *The Times*, *l'Express*, *Les Temps Modernes*, *Time* magazine or the *New York Times*, which are suppressed when carrying news on Portuguese affairs. These are copied on privately owned duplicating machines and distributed at the expense of small groups of people who run tremendous risks for their efforts. Even abroad, Portuguese politicians sometimes hardly have money to eat, let alone finance expensive plots. The seizure of the *Santa Maria* was part of a larger plan for the simultaneous seizure of three liners in different parts of the world, a scheme which would have involved an investment of some £10,000, but this sum was never found.

With the £3,000 which *was* collected and saved, the conspirators managed to buy old-fashioned guns and third-class tickets and off they went to make the loudest possible propaganda with their limited resources. They timed their coup to coincide with the change in the American administration on 20th January and the forthcoming inauguration of President Quadros in Brazil on 10th February. In this way they benefited from the natural hesitations of the new governments, preoccupied with the complicated matters of assuming power. President Kubitschek of Brazil was known to be pro-Salazar, in spite of the fact that Brazilians had been increasingly concerned with

Portuguese politics, not only as a result of the scandal of Delgado's asylum in Lisbon, but because of their growing interest in African affairs. He was known, for instance, to have meekly accepted Dr. Salazar's delays over Brazilian consular representation in Angola and Mozambique, where Brazil is likely to inherit the cloak of Portuguese cultural influence. President Quadros, on the other hand, had had an interview with Henrique Galvao in Venezuela and was known to entertain little of his predecessor's sympathy for the Lisbon Government.

At this favourable moment, a handful of conspirators went quietly on board the *Santa Maria* at the port of La Guaria, disguised as third-class passengers. The plans had been carefully prepared by a woman revolutionary on the staff of the ship, who had been jotting down the routine of the ship's officers so that all should go smoothly. The guns were introduced on board inside a coffin accompanied, in the interests of realism, by wailing women. Henrique Galvao himself embarked in the guise of a wealthy invalid.

When the moment of seizure arrived, the officers were too stunned to react, and only one of them, described by Galvao himself as a brave man, offered resistance and was killed. For the next few days the greatest secret on board was the real number of the conspirators. They had to keep appearing in rotation like a stage army, to make believe they were not seventeen but a hundred and seventy.

Like Galvao, some of the pirates were men who, in a normal country, would have been Members of Parliament, or respected pillars of society. Such people, it is clear, did not seize a liner in mid-ocean for the fun of it.

As intended, the rich Press of the democratic world duly financed the publicity of the impoverished fighters for freedom. In fact, some magazines and newspapers spent more money in covering the affair then the *Movimento Nacional Independente* could afford to spend on the action itself. General Delgado went on board the *Santa Maria*, when it was lying off Recife, as a guest of *Time* magazine reporters, who had rented a boat for the purpose. Brazilian students collected the money to take care of the conspirators, who had not only exhausted all their meagre finances, but left behind a number of signed but unpaid bills in the bar of the ship. There had clearly been no money from Moscow behind *this* revolutionary enterprise!

For the Portuguese, the incident had a profound psychological meaning. Henrique Galvao, in his younger days, had been one of the bravest fighters for the establishment of the present regime in Portugal, and an upholder of Salazar's view that the Right should try to carry out a reform in Portuguese life lest the Left be called upon to do so. That he should, thirty-three years later, become one of the fiercest opponents of the regime and one of the most outspoken leftist radicals was in itself lasting proof of the failure of Dr. Salazar's attempt at reforming Portugal. The irony is even more far reaching. While Dr. Salazar, by allowing a free contest for the 120 seats at the National Assembly in the forthcoming elections (due to take place in October 1961), may be able to obtain a certain measure of collaboration from the moderates, and thus divide the Democrats, the *Movimento Nacional Independente*, led as it is by two former Estado Novo supporters, is a no-nonsense revolutionary movement aiming at a complete reform of the social structure of Portugal, without which any political change can only end up as just another form of dictatorship, more or less disguised in a framework of paternalism.

While much is to be expected of their actions in the future, Delgado and Galvao remain two formidable figures in Portuguese politics. Dr. Salazar's principal disciples are too unpopular and too deeply compromised with the present regime to hope for any measure of popular support in Portugal. Even the Democratic leaders are dismissed as being too intellectual and too old by the largely ignorant Portuguese masses. Only Delgado and Galvao command a nation-wide measure of popularity amongst the people. Their spectacular high-seas adventure introduced into Portuguese politics the novel spirit and methods of the revolution of Fidel Castro, whose influence is powerful throughout Latin America, where the Portuguese opposition leaders and their supporters are now reunited in exile.

The *Santa Maria*, temporarily renamed the *Santa Liberdade*, may not have got to Africa as first intended, but it certainly succeeded in creating a background of world attention for the forgotten issue of Portuguese politics, and its seizure was the precursor of a whole chain of events not only inside Portugal but throughout the Empire.

Chapter VII

METAPHYSICAL COLONIALISM

The Empire without Imperialism

IN THE SLOW pace of life of the fifteenth century the Portuguese, confined to the western coastal belt of the Iberian Peninsula, wondered what could possibly lie beyond the sea horizon. Monsters were said to rise from the bed of the ocean. There were rumours that, far away across the sea, night was permanent and the sky devoid of stars. The earth being flat, one would be faced with a sudden void. Some enterprising Portuguese decided that their horizons of curiosity and expansion should be challenged. And so they studied and worked and challenged the unknown, and in the process added to human achievement. This achievement can be measured by the fact that the Portuguese nation, then scarcely comprising more than one and a quarter million people, extended its activities half way across the globe—across the Atlantic into Brazil and the New World, around the extreme south of Africa to India, China and Japan. Exploring Africa centuries before any other Europeans, Portuguese pioneers undoubtedly planted there the first seeds of civilization and introduced crops which form the staple foods of most Africans today. What came afterwards was not their fault.

Most of the pioneers of the Portuguese discoveries are forgotten in the Estado Novo's historical reverie. The figures that animate official history are those of the Empire-builders. The Estado Novo's colonial mystique is largely based on what they wrote: an amalgam of convenient tenets which may have been modern three or four centuries ago.

The process of Portuguese imperialism was already well advanced when, in 1684, the Viceroy of India issued an edict that "it is no less desirable that the natives of the country abandon the use of their language and all begin to speak the Portuguese language. . . . It will be easier for the priest to catechise and instruct in the mysteries of the faith . . . I assign to them the time of three years within which all shall speak the Portuguese idiom . . ." But even in those times the idea of building an empire bound by a common language and religion met with resistance and difficulty. Fifty years later the Inquisitor of India, calling for other measures to be adopted, remarked in a report to the Portuguese king, "the first and foremost cause of this pitiful ruin of souls is the non-observance of the law . . . that forbids the natives to speak their language and compels them to speak only Portuguese . . ." In the same report he added a revealing passage: "From this non-observance resulted many great evils and irreparable damages to their souls and to the royal estates of Your Majesty."

In the twentieth century the Portuguese oligarchy, organized into the Estado Novo, tried to revive the doctrines of Portuguese imperial literature, as if the pace and conditions of life in the modern age had not outdated the doctrines of mediaeval imperialism.

Today the bulk of the overseas population of the "nation" does not speak Portuguese and remains pagan. An indication of the results of the civilizing mission is given by the *Anuario Estatistico do Ultramar* (*Lisbon Instituto Nacional de Estatistica*, 1959) in the following figures from the last available census (1950):

Territory	Uncivilized	Civilized	Percentage
Guinea	502,457	1,478	0.29
Sao Thomé	16,747	37,950[1]	70.00
Angola	4,006,598	30,089	0.74
Mozambique	5,646,957	25,149	0.44
Timor	434,907	1,541	0.35
	10,607,666	96,207	0.90

The Empire comprises a number of separate and distant territories which are bound together, not by sentiment and theory, but, like all other empires, in proportion to their economic development and wealth. There is hardly any communication between Portugal and Goa (in India), Timor (in the East Indies) and Macau (in China).

[1] The Sao Thomé Africans are not governed by the "Native Statute" and therefore are considered citizens on a par with Metropolitan Portuguese. The figure for "uncivilized" is made up of imported forced labourers from other African territories.

Nearer home, the Cape Verde islands lie forgotten in mid-ocean off the west coast of Africa and very little is done to solve their acute and chronic social problems, including an endemic state of famine. The introduction of Guinea and the Sao Thomé islands to the Portuguese way of life is confined to the teaching of the mysteries of export and import rather than those of the faith. Political developments outside these small territories have reduced most of them to the status of geographical oddities.

The Empire is Angola and Mozambique, which together cover an area the size of Western Europe. In spite of their underdeveloped condition, their trade and budgets are rapidly overtaking those of Portugal itself.

The overwhelming majority of Africans who inhabit these territories have hardly been touched by civilization or, more precisely, by the benefits of civilization. Out of ten and a half million people (Angola 4,500,000: Mozambique six million), over ninety-nine per cent are illiterate. Less than four per cent in Mozambique and less than eight per cent in Angola know how to speak Portuguese at all. Less than five per cent in Mozambique and less than ten per cent in Angola live in or around the white man's towns, the only centres where some development is achieved by the natural process of social contact. If there has been any serious interest in these people it has been in how better to shape their lives to economic exploitation.

Portuguese and foreign students of African affairs, misled by the talk of "assimilation", have come to think that the "assimilado" system has been devised to give Africans the rights of citizenship. At first sight, by contrast with other colonial policies, the idea that Africans, after meeting with some qualifications, could earn the "generous concession" of citizen rights looks stimulating. But assimilation, "partnership" and their friendly opposite, "apartheid", are all features of colonialist mythology. The white man cannot ignore the realities of African demography, and out of moral and political necessity he finds elaborate theories which he applies more or less to suit himself.

While the feasibility of apartheid in its absolute form is doubtful, and partnership clearly aims at maintaining the white man's position as managing-director of the association, the fallacy of "assimilation" is that the assimilados are hardly anywhere to be found (even from statistical data they are absent, since the Portuguese Government has lately seen to it that no figures are released). According to the latest known count, less than one in a hundred Africans in Angola and less than a half per cent in Mozambique had attained the rights of citizens. These rights do not in any case carry them very far, since even the Portuguese themselves have few rights under the Estado Novo, and the concession of rights promised in the *assimilado* system is tantamount to the recognition that Africans do not naturally enjoy *any*. In point of fact, the *Estatuto dos Indigenas* (Native Statute), under which the remaining ninety-nine per cent of population in Angola and ninety-nine and a half per cent of the population in Mozambique are ruled, reduces Africans to the condition of wards of the administration—a condition that is convenient for the exploitation of the territories' greatest wealth, that of African labour.

Under this same statute the African populations of Angola and Mozambique, which have been sporadically disturbed in their huts and fields since time immemorial, have been increasingly interfered with of recent years by the white man. Their lives are still socially primitive, but their ancestral fear of wild animals has long been equalled by the fear of running into trouble with the omniscient Administration. Theirs is a small walking-distance world, in which the tribal witch-doctor competes with the *missionarios*—normally white priests, dressed in long white cassocks, who often talk to Africans about love and brotherhood, but are seriously embarrassed to give any visual and practical examples of it. However, not even what the Africans hear about Christ, who appears to them as a white man, and therefore not fully to be trusted, eliminates their fear of foreign intrusion. The imagination of most Africans is filled with suspicion. They still hear stories of their ancestors who disappeared after having been hunted like animals at a time coinciding with that of slavery. Their ignorance of written language, the limited vocabularies of their own dialects, their social backwardness, all make them impenetrable to any form of political propaganda, except that based on the affinities, the sufferings and grievances of their race. Most of them have never heard of the United States, the Soviet Union or the United Nations. Some still wonder whether there are more blacks than whites in Africa. All they can see is that African kraals have very few people, while there are big towns, populated by white people who have cars nearly as big as their huts and houses as high as mountains. The framework of European technological civilization is in itself enough to intimidate them.

Poor Africans! In administrative districts often inhabited, according to estimates, by over thirty thousand people, with a territorial area the size of European counties, a white administrative official is the only authority. Isolation and absolute power is a challenge to character. Administrative Officers, in spite of the best of individual intentions, cannot escape the prejudices of their Portuguese outlook, which has been shaped back in Europe by a set of political values that turns even Portuguese citizens into serfs. Known and punished abuses of their powers of administrative "paternalism" (in the circumstances, a negligible proportion of those practised) have included most forms of moral corruption and brutality. Extreme cases have involved beatings to the point of permanent injury. On over thirty charges, one of them being the arbitrary arrest of a family, including the husband, for the sake of enjoying the nubile charms of a young African woman, an official in Mozambique was punished with the purely administrative sanction of suspension from duty. Even where a case might be brought against an administrative official it meets with a number of difficulties. For one thing, the judicial framework of both Angola and Mozambique only applies to the minority of "civilized" people (some 230,000 in Angola and 120,000 in Mozambique, of whom the majority are white): for another, and consequently, courts only exist in the towns, which are scattered hundreds of miles apart, and mainly along the coast.

The technicalities of immunity are such that administrative officials can always justify the application of sanctions on grounds of having been "disrespected". The principle of "respect" towards these officers, both in their capacity as white men and as "representatives of Portugal", makes everything possible. If an African is ordered to cultivate some inedible crop in which he is not interested, or is pressed into directed labour and resists authority, he is liable to punishment. If he keeps annoying the Administration with a just protest over a very human grievance (such as that of the husband mentioned above), and in the process loses his humble composure in addressing the administrative official, he is liable to punishment. The palmatoria, a five-holed wooden instrument like a ping-pong bat, with which Africans are beaten on the palms of their hands or, less frequently, on the soles of their feet, is used as a deterrent in the case of petty offences. Order is maintained essentially through corporal punishment: prisons would be too expensive either to build or to run. A major offence or crime provides the State with a forced labourer, who has to work without pay for an indefinite period of time, either for the local Administration, or in distant labour camps inside Angola, or in Sao Thomé to which Africans are regularly deported.

There is hardly any place left to which to escape from the Administration. Administrative officials have cars which cover in a matter of hours distances which Africans take days to cover on foot. African administrative policemen, dressed in khaki, often come to bring them to the white *senhores chefes de posto* and *administradores* (administrative officials and district commissioners). All white men appear to Africans to have one thing in common: an obsession with work, work. Even the white priests, under the pretext of giving agricultural teaching, or as a mode of collecting teaching fees and payment for books and school materials, make money out of African children, who are induced to work in small, well-kept plantations adjoining the missions. One of the principle causes of unrest leading up to the recent troubles, especially in Angola, was the forced labour system which upset the family life of the Africans as well as the cultivation of their own subsistence crops. The practice in recent years has taken two main forms. One is that Africans have been forced to grow cash crops in commercial demand, which are sold to neighbouring stores or seasonal markets. The Government having a vested interest in production, the administrative officials are instructed to supervise the crops, which are sold to private concessionaries for later export to Portugal. According to the amount of production in his area, which will eventually be reflected in the turnover of tax collection, the administrative official can assure himself of a number of advantages, such as increased chances of promotion and discreet rewards from the concessionary companies themselves. Exploitation reaches appalling proportions, and the cotton trade is a good example.

In the organised concessionary buying markets, held in strategic Administrative centres, white employees of these companies, under the eyes of the friendly white officials who are supposed to act as inspectors, weigh and pay for the cotton. On a sort of conveyor-belt system, Africans queue up to get some coins and pieces of paper called money in exchange for their produce. The queue then immediately proceeds until it reaches the Administrative officers. There, on the spot, those who have just been paid leave a considerable part of their money to pay the *imposto* (the tax), which has at times been called the "hut tax", the "native tax", and now the "individual tax".

For the sake of simplification, all pay the same fixed sum. Since cotton is bought from them at an average of ninepence a kilo, it takes a great volume and weight of cotton to make up the levy, which varies from £1 to £1 10s., according to the specific area of concession. A total of over 500,000 African growers is currently engaged in cotton production in Mozambique alone. By dividing the total amount that concessionaries pay to African growers, their annual income per head is seen to average about £5. This is in compensation for a full year's work on compulsory crops while their own food crops are neglected. The Government's proud boast that a handful of Africans have earnings in excess of £70 a year only makes one wonder how many Africans work the year round almost solely to pay the individual tax.

The other form of forced labour surviving into the mid-twentieth century is the *contracto* system—an abusive euphemism, since Africans, being mostly illiterate, could not any way understand its implications. Under this system, all available "idle" men between the apparent ages of fourteen and sixty—few Africans are ruled by the calendar, and the counting of age is irrelevant to them—are liable to be engaged under contract. The definition of "idle" is logically applied to those who are not working, i.e. mostly those who are not already under *contracto*. To Africans this means being forced to leave land and family and to work, in some cases, hundreds of miles from home, regardless of climatic and other differences, such as a change in staple diet. In order to implement this system of *contracto* labour, the Administration provide the apparatus of co-ordination, recruitment and supply. In other words, to meet public or private requirements that are notified to the authorities, administrative agents, mostly Africans, go hunting for able-bodied men. These men are taken to the Administration and detained. If there is no immediate transport available, they are kept there until they can be loaded into lorries to white-owned plantations, farms and factories, or to the work sites of Government-operated public services, railways, ports and departments of public works. These are often in an entirely different region, inhabited by other Africans whose language and culture are alien to them. Only the practice of housing the imported workers in segregated compounds saves them from being completely lost in an entirely strange social milieu, and this factor alone invalidates all possibility of escape. Normally such contracts are valid for six months and the wages, ranging from 25s. to £2 a month, are kept until the term of employment expires. The duration of the *contracto* and this retention of wages, assures, among other things, that taxes are paid in due time when the labourers return to their respective administrative areas.

Africans are of course unaware of what is happening to them. Such theories as the "dignity of labour" and "civilizing through work" can only be taken seriously by those who have a vested interest in self-deception. Under the forced *contracto* system, Africans end up with a varied set of experiences such as six months' training in trades ranging from sugar-cane cutting to road making, public construction, railway shunting, stevedoring and ditch-digging, and alternation between subsistence economy and *contracto* labour has ensured that they remain a source of cheap labour, as unskilled today as it has always been.

Over the years, the system has, of course, resulted in social changes. By a comprehensible phenomenon of human adaptation to prevailing conditions, an increasing number of Africans have taken the initiative and become volunteer workers—not because current wages and working conditions are particularly rewarding, but because they are left with no alternative. They then emigrate, either to other African and foreign countries or to the urban centres.

As in all Southern Africa, their wider contact with the white man's life still gives little or no opportunity for social uplift. They become domestic servants, casual labourers, street cleaners, nurse-maids, cooks—with average salaries ranging from £1 5s. to £4 a month. Some rise to positions as office-boys and clerks, a career which can pay as much as £30 a month—the lowest rate on the white man's scale. A number of enterprising Africans manage to attain the self-employment category as shoe-shiners and cobblers, carpenters, car-washers, gardeners, and so on.

Except for the domestic servants, who live in backyard rooms, Africans generally return after work to their own locations, conveniently situated around the white men's towns. They soon become adjusted to the pattern of segregated life. Racial discrimination is disguised under many subtle subterfuges. At the Post Office, for instance, "Telegrams handed by the Bearer" and "Telegrams handed by the Sender" notices are the Portuguese equivalents of "Whites Only" and "Blacks Only": but racial discrimination is all-pervading.

For Africans, towns represent the world of the pass book and the curfew. Revelling in the efficiency of the pass book, the Administrator of Lourenço Marques almost managed to write a masterpiece of

subversive propaganda: "The pass book is an interesting document...
it is a kind of biographical register of great utility which allows one
in a few moments to know everything in connection with him [the
African]... For the employer this is an extraordinary facility...
No native can ever be admitted to work if he does not possess a pass
book, or if the pass book does not show clearly that he is free to be
employed, and authorized to stay in the city."[1]

But the existence of urban minorities and other exceptional cases
does not invalidate the fact that forced labour has provided the basis
of the economy both in Angola and Mozambique. "We need the
labour of the natives. We need it in order to improve the conditions
of the labourers themselves; we need it for the economy of Europe
and for the progress of Africa. Capital... needs workers in abundance
who are sturdy and cheap..."[2] writes a Portuguese colonialist,
though it is a moot point whether even the white Angola and Mozambique settlers really profit from the system, which is used mostly in
connection with export crops in the hands of Metropolitan capital
interests. There would be much to gain from an increase in the purchasing power of Africans, the potential customers of local industry.

While fulfilling the requirements of the first school of thought
the Estado Novo has used its censorship machine to conceal the forced
labour system from the public both in Portugal and the world at
large, but censorship cannot be absolutely effective. It does not hide
the truth from Africans, who do not read. All they can see of the
"Portuguese soul" is what is done in its name—all the comparative
theories of a distinctive Portuguese character, supposedly exempt from
racial prejudice, however true in respect of community relations, are
contradicted by their long and painful experience in this field. They
are not to know that the treatment conferred upon them does not
differ from that of their counterparts in Portugal. Unlike that of most
of the theorists who take the liberty of speaking on their behalf, the
world of the overwhelming majority of Africans within Portuguese
Africa is a small world, inhabited by black workers and white bosses.
Since the good bosses in Portuguese Africa, as indeed in all Southern
Africa, are the exception rather than the rule, grievances begin to
follow a racial pattern. Africans throughout the centuries, long before

[1] Speech at International Administrative Congress, Durban, 1956, quoted in
Harris, *Portugal's African Wards*.

[2] Antonio Enes, *Moçambique*, Agencia Geral das Colonias, Lisbon, 1946.

nationalism became a fashionable issue and found written doctrines of its own, have intuitively discovered the nature of the white man's presence in their land. Passive resistance has been a widespread phenomenon. The so-called *perguiça*, or laziness, of Africans, contradicted as it is by the massive emigratory trends to neighbouring territories and in many other ways, is an expression of a collective, although inarticulate, nativist attitude of non-collaboration. Wages on *contracto* labour, as well as earnings from marketed crops, are so low, and relatively so decreased by taxation, that Africans would rather be left to their subsistence economy than work for the white man. The whole situation that first led to forced labour is an expression of passive resistance. Negligence, desertion, even sheer sabotage, are much in evidence. The administrative sanctions, harsh as they may be in cases of non-payment of taxes, are not enough guarantee that Africans will work to meet them. A constant supervision of crops is required: Africans often hide or run away. In the process of keeping the system going, abuses and acts of violence occur. While censorship may prevent the Portuguese people and the world from being fully informed of these practices, there is obviously no way of hiding them from the victims and those who have deserted to neighbouring countries are now organizing and waging a war against the Portuguese.

It is no use making cases against individual administrative officials. There are many of them who deplore the existing methods and conditions. The case should be brought against the administrative system as a whole. The susceptibilities on the issue of forced labour are such that the Statute of Native Labour in Mozambique included in one of its paragraphs a sudden and puzzling sanction to the effect that whoever criticizes labour laws contained therein as constituting slavery, or in any way whatsoever contributes to the discredit of the authorities, is liable to two years in jail, a fine of £250 and banishment from the territory.

Forced labour as it has been known recently in Portuguese Africa is in a category by itself. The niceties of a comparative analysis as between this system and slavery are, however, purely academic. Under the system of slavery that shipped men to the New World and which is most often evoked in such comparisons, the expenditure involved in recruitment and transport to the coast of Africa and across the ocean was quite considerable. Ownership of the slave was therefore essentially a method of guaranteeing the capital investment. In Portuguese Africa today such investment is not required. Africans are there in plentiful quantity. They look after themselves and the soil of Africa feeds the old among them and the children. But the essential moral point is the same—that forced labour, in whatever form, is an infringement of human rights. While the element of private ownership of the individual slave is lacking, one can say that the use of the administrative apparatus to facilitate practices that have little regard for written laws has amounted to the collective ownership of a population by the colonial administration. These immense territories, hardly traversed by anybody except the Administrative Officers and the Africans, become reserves of cheap human labour exploited by the white man's enterprises as an inexhaustible pool.

Nothing that is morally wrong can be politically right, and there is yet another dangerous affinity between the new-style forced labour and the old slavery system. In economic perspective, slavery as a source of labour was the basis of an economy. The abolition of slavery brought with it uprisings, the seizure of ships on the high seas and even wars. When it eventually came to be enforced, many companies went bankrupt. So entrenched was the system that wherever it prevailed it left its seeds of social differentiation. Even today in the southern United States conditions of labour for foreign immigrants fall below those prevailing all over the rest of the country. In Portuguese Africa, where forced labour has long been used by private companies as well as Government services, the economy is dangerously compromised with the system. It may be nominally relaxed in the face of international criticism today, but its sudden total abolition would mean more than a reduction of profits for most enterprises and services whose establishment and operation are based on estimates of wages that only forced labour conditions could allow. In a sort of chain reaction, it would mean that production of most export commodities would cease. Monies earned by Africans, little as they are, keep internal trade going: the products of forced labour keep the railways and shipping moving. Government services themselves, employing forced labourers as they do, would be simultaneously paralysed by the desertion of many employees. The African population of Portuguese Africa, divided as it was formerly into many languages and tribes, has now, by opposition to the white ruler and by the common link of oppression acquired its own unity.

The Emigrants turn Rebels

One of the most eloquent expressions of African resistance to forced labour and oppression is the rate of emigration from Portuguese territories.

Emigration is a feature common to all parts of the Empire. Nearly 600,000 Portuguese have emigrated from Europe, mostly to Brazil, since the establishment of the Estado Novo. From Madeira and the Azores thousands travel, often clandestinely, to South Africa and the United States to join friends and relatives who have long been settled there. To the misery-oppressed Cape Verde islanders emigration is the only escape. They come mostly to the west coast of Africa. Not only do they settle in Portuguese Guinea, but they join Guineans in crossing the border to neighbouring territories. Eighty thousand Goans, some fifteen per cent of the Goan population, live in Bombay, as well as other parts of India, Pakistan and the east coast of Africa. The number of Goans employed by almost all shipping lines cruising the Pacific and Indian Oceans provides a fluctuating community of catering and laundry specialists. Most educated Portuguese from Macau work and live in neighbouring Hong Kong, or take up jobs in Singapore and nearly all the ports of Japan. Even the natives of Timor, near Australia, are not immune from the lure of better possibilities on the Dutch half of the island. Though oppressive rule has in some cases been an additional incentive, in these cases the trends can be said to follow the pattern of social underdevelopment. The rate of emigration from Angola and Mozambique cannot be so easily dismissed, and Portuguese experts, Henrique Galvao amongst them, are aware of its relation to the forced labour system.

Such is the scale of this social phenomenon in Portuguese Africa that studies on the subject can only be conjectural. Portuguese authors of suppressed books have estimated that over one million people from Mozambique have settled in Nyasaland alone, largely to escape the rigours of the *prazos* system, when the territory was divided into concessions to private companies which were given sovereign rights for the economic exploitation of the land and its people. This factor may help to explain why Nyasaland has a greater density of population than any other territory in the same geo-political area. According to Professor Marcelo Caetano's *Os nativos na Economia Africana*[1], the

[1] Coimbra, 1954.

number of Portuguese Africans living outside Mozambique and Angola can be estimated at over five hundred thousand for each territory, but some experts disagree on these figures, stating that a million for each would be a more accurate estimate. Curiously enough, so clear is this problem that African delegates at the United Nations, in their fierce attacks on the Estado Novo, content themselves with a conservative estimate of 250,000 for Angola.

Although these tides of emigration to foreign centres of economic development have their counterpart in other territories of Southern Africa, namely the British protectorates, the fact that in both Angola and Mozambique only geo-physical barriers hamper the steady flow of traditional emigration is indicative of a widespread feeling of revolt against the ubiquitous forced labour system and against all the acts of violence perpetrated in the course of its enforcement. From Angola, Africans have settled in the former French and Belgian Congos, as well as in Northern Rhodesia and South West Africa. From Mozambique, emigration to South Africa is not entirely in the direction of the Transvaal: it is extensive to the Province of Natal. Emigration to the Federation flows into Southern Rhodesia and over the Nyasaland frontiers, reaching far inland to Northern Rhodesia and, on a smaller scale, across the dividing Ruvuma river, into Tanganyika.

But Africans in the border regions are not always attracted by wages, and are often content to settle with their families on empty land on the other side of the frontier. Here, with luck, they manage to escape taxation or conscription by the Portuguese Administration. After leaving their tribal homes in Angola and Mozambique, and still untouched by the white man's culture, the immigrants, in the course of their employment in English and French speaking firms and households, and through contact with other Africans, often become integrated into the local communities. Africans of Mozambique origin who speak English are nearly as many as Mozambique Africans who speak Portuguese, and there are thousands of French-speaking Angolans who are indistinguishable from French or Belgian Congolese (a fact which disposes of the official claim that trouble-matters in the recent Angolan disturbances were foreigners because they spoke French).

These facts are not taught to Portuguese school children, primary or otherwise; they are suppressed as every other fact that may cloud the official image of the Empire is suppressed. A taboo has been imposed on discussion of any aspect of colonial policies—a taboo which extends even to that period of electoral campaigning when a limited freedom of speech on domestic issues is allowed. It is significant that the Galvao report[1] led to the imprisonment not only of the author but of some of the people involved in its circulation, and that even such experts on overseas affairs as Mr. Cunha Leal have had to limit themselves to a tentative approach to the subject of colonial administration in which their views were more implicit than expressed. But Dr. Salazar must have been thinking of the problem of the Portuguese African settlements in neighbouring countries when, in a speech analysing the political situation of Portugal and its Empire, long before the "wind of change" phrase was coined, he hinted at Communist subversion, remarking that "the fire was fed from outside". The Portuguese administrative authorities and the Portuguese Security Police must have reported that the sporadic agitation throughout the Portuguese Empire was in some way connected with returning emigrants. Reports on incidents in Sao Thomé, Guinea, Angola, Mozambique and Goa revealed a common pattern: in spite of the effectiveness of Police and administrative rules, ideas, comparisons and contrasts still filtered through in the course of family and social exchanges between visiting or returning emigrants and their people. Furthermore, some of those returning to Mozambique and Angola were said to be well trained agents, from Communist schools in Moscow and Prague, specialized in spreading revolutionary propaganda at a tribal level. It was, in fact, as we shall see, to be amongst the large African settlements in other territories that the Portuguese revolutionary movements in Angola would recruit and organize uprisings against the Portuguese

It is not to be denied, therefore, that whatever government is to succeed the Estado Novo in Portuguese Africa, be it a liberal Portuguese government, a local white-dominated or non-racial government, or a government of African nationalists, will be faced with a hard task of correcting the structural errors of the present system.

Whatever the consequences, African populations must, in the name of civilization, be freed as soon as possible from a situation that wastes the vitality of human beings in conditions that cannot meet with the approval of men of conscience. The individual problems of the huge Portuguese African territories must therefore be faced squarely before it is too late.

[1] See Appendix II.

Chapter VIII

MOZAMBIQUE

Economic Realities

WHEN THINKING OF Mozambique one must look at the map of
Africa. The territory, which lies forgotten on the south-eastern coast
of Africa, covering an area roughly the size of Great Britain and France
put together, is strategically one of the most important of Southern
Africa. Its 1,250 miles of seaboard, extending northwards from South
Africa's province of Natal to Tanganyika, is the natural coast for the
whole economic centre of the white-dominated south. The landlocked hinterland served by the ports of Lourenço Marques and Beira
ranges from the gold-rich Rand to copper-rich Katanga, across the
Federation of Rhodesia and Nyasaland. Some fifty per cent of all the
seaborne traffic of the Transvaal, some ninety per cent of the Federation's foreign trade and even some of Katanga's exports of mineral
raw materials are handled at Mozambique ports. An annual average of
ten million tons of rich cargo are carried on Mozambique railways on
their way to and from the ports of Lourenço Marques and Beira, where
loading and unloading operations go on the year round and around
the clock. The future of Mozambique is therefore of vital importance
to the political destinies of the southern African states.

Such is the impact of the neighbourhood of prosperous South Africa
and the Federation that Mozambique earnings from railway and port
services and from the supply of African labour and tourism currently
exceed the income that is earned by its exports, twenty per cent of
which also find their way into South Africa and the Federation. The
budgetary item *Consignaçao de Receitas* (Consignment of Revenue), to
which the railways and ports administration revenue at over £25
million accrues, accounts for nearly half of the entire budget.

While its geographical position has determined most of Mozambique's economic development and is shaping the pattern of its social
life, internal economic and social achievements do not match its

decisive political role. The African population of over six million people is under the control of seventy thousand whites who in their turn are under the rule of the Estado Novo. By remote dictatorial control from Lisbon, these people are kept divided into two separate worlds: the Africans plunged into illiteracy and ignorance, the whites cocooned in censorship and myth.

The white population is the most socially advanced Portuguese community in the world, the black the most backward in all the Portuguese territories of Africa. The standard of living of the whites is much higher than that prevailing in Portugal itself, and almost on a par with that of neighbouring South African and Rhodesian populations. Having brought with them European notions of nationality, Mozambique settlers and Mozambique-born whites have an incipient nationalism or separatism of their own, which the oppressive rule of the Estado Novo has done much to intensify.

Politically, Mozambique is the testing-ground of the Estado Novo's much advertised, centuries-old colonial philosophy of a non-racial "civilizing mission". This meets here with the challenge of the more blunt and modern facts of "apartheid"—a natural phenomenon which, in Mozambique, is automatically provided by the Estado Novo's repressive colonial system and dictatorial methods that simultaneously proclaim the ideals of non-racialism and invalidate any political intercourse between whites, let alone between whites and blacks.

The Portuguese Government has a vested interest in this form of sleep. The Estado Novo is determined that Mozambique shall remain, like Angola, a white-dominated "Province" of Portugal, not only in order to assure the continuance of Metropolitan Portugal's sovereignty, but as a way of complying with the all-pervading diplomatic pressures of both South Africa and the Federation.

Lest politically vulnerable Mozambique should eventually become an African state, and thus further isolate and jeopardize the survival of South Africa's dream of "apartheid", South African ministers have publicly expressed the desire that Mozambique should increase its white population. This desire unmasks two things: on the one hand, the inconsistencies of the "apartheid" doctrine (for if the drama of "apartheid" is the result of white presence in Africa, South Africans should rather urge Europeans to stay at home . . . in Europe); on the other, South Africa's appreciation of the true nature of "assimilation" as a colonialist expedient, only supposed to exist in theory. Far from

Angola and Mozambique in relation to the industrial heart of Africa

being disturbed by the threat implied in the "assimilation" system, which, if seriously applied, could lead to the political domination of Mozambique by the African, Afrikaners state bluntly that they believe the British in Rhodesia and the Portuguese in their African territories will alike be forced to adopt "apartheid" officially, as soon as social and political conditions are ripe. The Federation, whose "partnership" scheme is in essence closely related to "assimilation", puts a similar form of pressure on Mozambique, anxious as she is to maintain control over her natural outlet to the sea.

Meanwhile the Portuguese in Mozambique bury their heads in the sand. One of the facts most carefully kept out of public discussion is that of its demographic reality. While white South Africans are out-numbered one to three, white Southern Rhodesians one to ten and white Angolans one to twenty, Mozambique whites are outnumbered by one to a hundred. Analysis of the population censuses reveals that, in one year alone, the natural growth of the African population, at some eighty thousand people, is greater than the total existing white population. Even if economic expansion were to allow for an increase in the annual rate of growth in the white population, it is unlikely that in the foreseeable future whites could substantially reduce the margin by which they are outnumbered. A full study of the impli-cations of this basic problem would clarify all aspects of policy in Mozambique, even for those who are responsible for them.

In a race against time, great efforts are being made to increase the white population. In the period 1950 to 1955, it increased from 48,213 to 67,485. The current annual rate of increase is some nine per cent, immigration being of course the main factor. Since Mozambique is following the social patterns of southern Africa as a whole, a high standard of living—apartheid's natural barrier—must be maintained. Unlike South Africa and the Federation, however, Mozambique's only economic resources are agricultural and "geographical" wealth, and therefore its development is almost entirely confined to expansion of existing activities, and the policy is to use this limited economic expansion to absorb new white population, rather than in making any real attempt to promote the social and economic development of Africans. But even this narrow goal is obstructed in many directions.

The Mozambique economy can be said to fall into two main parts: one of these is formed by its export trade, which currently earns an average of some £25 million. But exports only pay for about fifty per cent of imports, the gap being partly caused, as is to be expected, by a disproportionate expenditure on equipment required for the maintenance and constant expansion of the ports and railway services. Deferred pay and remittances from an estimated 300,000 Africans, working either legally or illegally in the Transvaal and Rhodesian mines and industries, and the proceeds of tourism (over 60,000 sea-seeking white inlanders from South Africa and the Rhodesias visit Mozambique every year) bridge the trade gap of over £18 million and, at the same time, meet the deficit on payments to Metropolitan Portugal.

As we have seen, the Estado Novo has virtual control over Mozambique's economic life and this control is used to meet Metropolitan Portugal's pressing need for foreign currency—since her own annual trade deficit is in the region of £50 million. While prices for raw materials and foodstuffs are officially kept below world levels, and some commodities, such as cotton and sugar, are sold exclusively to Portugal, imports into Mozambique are subject to protective policies aimed at maintaining the market for Metropolitan Portuguese manufactures where these would otherwise meet with foreign competition. Mozambique, therefore, uses practically all the sterling that is left after covering its own trade gap to meet its considerable deficit on payments to Portugal. But this constant need for sterling inevitably leaves Portuguese colonial policies open to diplomatic pressures from South Africa and the Rhodesias, and, what is more, creates a situation whereby the burden of economic development, subject both to exploitation from Lisbon and to the expensive policy of increasing white immigration, falls on the poor, uncomprehending Africans.

The overwhelming majority of the local population provide for their own subsistence from their food crops of maize, beans, peanuts, manioc and ground-nuts. Generally speaking, both men and women work, the men doing the harder work of tilling the land, the women the simpler menial tasks involved in routine agriculture. The Government knows that any family dependants will be able to wrest a meagre living from the land. This and this alone makes possible the incredibly low rate of pay which Africans derive either from their forced crops or their labour under the *contracto* system. But African labour is the main factor behind the production of raw materials and foodstuffs for the export trade, and though the production and processing of sugar, tea and vegetable oils may have required considerable capital expenditure and know-how, this cannot be a moral justification for the scale of wages and prices imposed.

Cotton is produced in Mozambique in the northern areas, where lack of economic activity has not yet created a pressing need for *contracto* labour. These areas are divided into concessions given to white-owned companies, in some cases associated with textile companies operating in Portugal, the exclusive destination of cotton exports. Each African is assigned 1.2 acres of land on which to plant cotton, irrespective of the fact that ecological conditions, primitive tools and techniques are inadequate. The Bishop of Beira in a suppressed book aptly entitled *Anti-communist Order* has said: "Right at the outset I want to affirm that there are aspects of this activity which can only with difficulty be justified in the light of Christian sociology... What difference is there between the activities of these natives and those who work as contracted labourers on the farms? None. Or rather, a difference does exist: the contract labourers receive clothing, food and board; here, nothing of this is supplied; whether the farm produces or does not produce, the contract workers receive a salary; here they receive the price of the cotton if the seeding is successful, and in case it isn't, as occurs in bad years for this kind of crop, they receive nothing." Further evidence for the Bishop of Beira's case is unknowingly provided by Professor Quitanilha, the Head of Mozambique's Cotton Research Centre: "If Portugal had had to purchase abroad all the cotton that the textile industry has consumed in the last few years that would have meant an annual expenditure of currency in the order of £12 million a year; if we add to [the imports of raw cotton] other subsidiary cotton products [seeds, oils, husks, etc.] we realize that the development of cotton production brought to the national economy an increase of nearly £18 million."[1]

Apart from its contribution to the export trade and to all forms of economic activity in Mozambique, including the Government-operated services, African labour is even profitable to Mozambique when used abroad. Under the terms of a Portuguese-South African convention, the Transvaal Chamber of Mines is granted permission to recruit in Mozambique an average of 100,000 labourers a year. In exchange, the South Africans pay the Portuguese Government some £2 per labourer, allow the Portuguese to collect taxes in South

[1] Quoted in *Noticias*, Lourenço Marques, for 25.12.57.

Africa, and guarantee that a minimum forty-seven and a half per cent of the seaborne import traffic to the area of Johannesburg, as well as the export of 340,000 cases of citrus fruits, will pass through the Mozambique railways and be handled at the port of Lourenço Marques. Together with remittances from Africans working in Rhodesia, and non-conventional Africans working in South Africa, proceeds from African emigrants are among the important sources of foreign currency.

Assimilation on Trial

In spite of the fact that Africans are the serfs who keep the economy moving and expanding, not even the amounts paid by Africans in direct taxation revert to their benefit. The annual "Individual Tax", applying to all African males between the ages of eighteen and sixty, was raised twenty per cent in 1958, to rates varying from 90 escudos (£1 2s. 6d.) in the northernmost districts to 300 escudos (£3 15s.) in the southern districts, and these sums, representing from twenty to eighty per cent of their meagre subsistence-level incomes, make Mozambique Africans the most heavily taxed people in the world. The only two significant forms of Government expenditure that are directly applied to the welfare of the African section of the population are those in connection with the health and education services. While the former is one of the most inadequate, even by Africa's colonial standards, so that most public and private employers have themselves to provide medical assistance, which is confined to assuring that workers are kept fit for work, an analysis of the problem of education in Mozambique unveils some even more disturbing truths about the policies of the home government.

Out of a revenue estimated at over £2 million from the total of "Individual Tax" collected, only some £350,000, or one per cent of the budgetary expenditure, is given to the Catholic Missions, who have the monopoly of education in Mozambique. With a *per capita* expenditure of less than £1 a year per African child of school age, it is not surprising that the rate of illiteracy in Mozambique remains at over ninety-nine per cent.

In this testing ground of the assimilation system, up till the time of the 1961 alarm no efforts had been made to extend either rudimentary or selective education. This alone betrays the cynical irrelevance of the traditional Portuguese concept of a "colonial and civilizing" mission.

Theoretically, under the *assimilado* system, education is, amongst other things, the means that could lead to political power. At the time of the 1950 census, Africans could become citizens legally on a par with whites provided (a) they could speak Portuguese; (b) they did not practise the uses and customs characteristic of the native way of life; and (c) they had an occupation in commerce or industry, or possessed property from which a living could be earned. The census showed that there were 164,580 Mozambique Africans who knew how to speak Portuguese. Of these, 56,270 could read and write, which was more than the legal requirement.

Small as these figures may be compared with the total African population (5,646,958 in 1950), the fact is that whites in Mozambique numbered only 48,213, including foreign residents, children and women, most of whom, under Portuguese law, have no right to vote. As, therefore, the number of Africans theoretically qualifying for citizenship would greatly exceed the number of Portuguese, conveniently, the "assimilated" Africans numbered only 4,349. In the five years between 1950 and 1955, the increase in the number of *assimilados* was only 206, or an average of forty-one and a fifth per year.

Faced with the dilemma of fulfilling Portugal's "civilizing mission" while complying with the "apartheid" policies of the geo-political area upon which Mozambique is economically dependent, the Estado Novo cunningly decided in 1954 that the better solution was to try to dodge international interest and United Nations pressure with a number of subtle changes in an already ambiguously worded set of "assimilation" requirements. "Citizens", black or white, have few rights and opportunities under the Estado Novo anywhere, but, in view of the fact that the minority of African citizens could easily outnumber the citizens of the numerically negligible white population, the Estado Novo's law-makers almost exhausted their literary imagination in the drafting of a new set of "assimilation" requirements. These were legalized in the *Estatuto dos Indigenas Portugueses das Provincias da Guine, Angola e Mozambique*. Conditions for "assimilation" were raised far above those implied in the earlier legislation. Africans were now required to speak Portuguese—*correctly*. It was no longer sufficient that they should break drastically with their own background and abandon "the customs and uses characteristic of the native way of life"; the evolution of these customs and uses should, on the contrary, be stimulated so as to form the essence of their own personality as a people. They were required to demonstrate that they had achieved "the learning and habits which are presupposed for the integral application of Portuguese private and public law". The assessment of these qualifications was conveniently left to the whim of the Administration. The comparatively large numbers of urban Africans who earn wages, speak and write Portuguese, have been converted to Catholicism and have adopted other European habits, fell henceforth into a category of sub-*assimilados*, for this is what current philosophizing on "partial cultural assimilation" really meant.

Since the definition of *correct* Portuguese can lead to heated discussions amongst Portuguese-born people themselves, according to their own regionalistic feelings, it is not surprising if foreign students of the African scene, not acquainted as we are with the Estado Novo, went on wasting their time trying to find out what the Government had done with the *assimilados*. They should have borne in mind that the Estado Novo's colonial policies are even more contradictory than those currently applied in Portugal itself. Indeed, the professed philosophy of the "civilizing mission", which is, so Portuguese school children are taught, a second *raison d'être* for the Portuguese nation, has often been contradicted in a simple phrase, even by leading figures of the regime. Professor Marcelo Caetano, a former Overseas Minister and Vice-Premier, who in this capacity ranked second only to Dr. Salazar in party hierarchy, stated in his book *Tradiços, Principios e Metodos da Colonizacao Portuguese*:[1] "Portugal does not accept in absolute terms the principles of the primacy of native interests."

The Crisis Looming

While the Portuguese rulers, on behalf of their inarticulate people, go on playing "colonial powers", hand in hand with South Africa and the Rhodesias, the six million Africans and the seventy thousand Mozambique whites are being trapped into a dramatic situation.

For the sake of elucidation, taking into account that the growth of the African population will increase in the future by a natural law of proportion, one could estimate that, towards the turn of this century only thirty years from now, the population of Mozambique will stand

[1] *Methods, Traditions and Principles of Portuguese Colonization*, Ministry of Overseas Affairs, 1957, page 41.

at something like 300,000 white people as opposed—and surely in more ways than one—to over eleven million Africans.

It is estimated that sixty per cent of the white population lives in Lourenço Marques (32,000) and Beira (18,000), and even amongst them there are a number of social inequalities, as is revealed by the fact that, while the average white man's salary in Mozambique is only £600 a year, the top income group includes ten thousand white settlers with annual incomes in excess of £1,200—even though, of course, the lion's share of Mozambique's business is in the hands of Metropolitan and British people who prefer to enjoy their profits in the cooler climate of Europe.

In their role as tourist resorts for South Africans and Rhodesians, these two towns, in contrast with the more isolated and smaller towns of Quelimane (5,000), Tete (3,000) and Nampula (2,500), provide a good example of the influence of economic conditions on the principle of non-racialism. In the hotels, boarding-houses and restaurants, Africans are only to be seen in the capacity of waiters, moreover, since the average salary of Africans does not exceed three shillings a day, which is less than the price of a cinema ticket, racial segregation is reinforced by a natural barrier—that of the inaccessibly high standard of living of the whites. It is ironical that, in spite of this striking contrast, and while these African wages are the lowest in the whole of southern Africa, even these rates, contrary to common belief, sometimes prevent competition with the outside world. Cashew nuts, for instance, are exported to India for shelling, before being re-exported to the United States, because to have this work done in Mozambique would be more expensive than the labour of Indian women. The Banco Nacional Ultramarino, in its Economic Review for 1956, quoted a report of the Directors of the Sociedade Algodoeira de Fomento Colonial, which owns a textile factory at Vila Pery, near Beira, stating that industrial labour costs work out higher in Mozambique than in Portugal itself—a fact that has greatly hampered industrial development in Portuguese Africa, since capital investment could only come from Portugal.

Apart from their economic advantages, the white community in the province, if only because it suits the colonial policies of the Estado Novo, has at present a position of apparent political power out of all proportion to its number. The Europeans can be said, in effect, to form a civilian occupation force. Africans are represented at the

Legislative Council by only two African Catholic priests, who are expected to say "amen" to everything as if they were permanently at Mass. Yet the political power of the whites is itself only relative, for their representatives are restricted to the supervision of specific economic and administrative matters. Major lines of policy are outlined in Portugal, and Dr. Salazar confines the rights of Legislative Councils in the African territories, as indeed of the National Assembly in Lisbon itself, to the discussion of legislation that does not involve any increase in public expenditure. Such indeed is the limitation of the powers of these Councils that the country might as well be openly ruled from Portugal.

European newcomers as they arrive in Africa soon fall into the well-established pattern of colonial life: they quickly adopt the accepted attitude that Mozambique is a "white man's country" where the black man is treated with that mixture of indifference and casual paternalistic affection peculiar to most Portuguese. The subservience of the Estado Novo to good neighbourly relations with South Africa is such that even doctrinaire criticisms of apartheid are suppressed by the censors. The State Police see to it that social intercourse between the two peoples goes no further than the usual routine exchanges between master and servant, and the average Mozambique white man is almost as unaware of the true situation as any Portuguese peasant at home. On the "I'm all right, Jack" principle he seldom looks below the surface. The Europeans cruising along the bougainvillaea-lined avenues of Lourenço Marques and Beira do not know that the "natives" who sweep the leaves from their beautiful pavements are forced labourers in the quite literal meaning of the phrase. When in this "Province" of the "one nation" isolated white Portuguese discover the nature of administrative practices, and attempt to protest in any way, they are summarily deported back to Portugal.

As for the Africans in Mozambique, their only hope of education and awakening formerly lay with the emigrants to South Africa and the Rhodesias. This hope no longer prevails, because of the close policy of collusion between the Portuguese authorities and their South African and Rhodesian counterparts. But there are large vulnerable stretches along the borders of Nyasaland, where, as we have seen, Mozambique Nyasas have settled on a massive scale, and the increasing agitation along this border seems to indicate that the eventual dissolution of the Federation would be followed by serious conflict in a large area of Mozambique. Although counter-measures have been taken, including the posting of white policemen equipped with machine-guns in the white-owned stores scattered throughout the frontier districts, such an eventuality would clearly be beyond police control. A handful of African political refugees in Kenya and Tanganyika have even formed parties under the auspices of local African political organizations and Goan patrons.

Yet, by one of the paradoxes of Portuguese politics, the small hard core of politicians in Mozambique itself, who have their own clandestine movements, is one of the most liberal that can be found anywhere in southern Africa. This is perhaps not surprising, since the Estado Novo in Portugal was in the habit of encouraging the quiet self-deportation of Metropolitan democrats to Mozambique until, following the elections of 1949, a large-scale, left-wing and multi-racial conspiracy was discovered there. A number of prominent liberals were arrested, and three of them (an engineer, a lady chemist and a lawyer) were deported back to Portugal and handed over to the PIDE in Lisbon.

To local politicians it seems that Mozambique, if it takes the opportunity, is in an excellent position to play an active role in the building of a non-racial southern Africa. They do not like apartheid, but nevertheless they can see in the growth of their own children how inevitable the phenomenon is in present social conditions. Race prejudice often appeals to Europeans in Africa as a way of justifying the existing social and economic inequalities. The white man, Portuguese or otherwise, grows accustomed to the inferior status of the coloured peoples and, despite the best of intentions, unconsciously forms the habit of seeing his social superiority as the result of inevitable natural circumstances. Racial prejudice thus tends to emerge out of social and economic prejudice. Unless the conditions of Africans are improved and they are given a greater part in the government of their own country, the whites will in fact be digging their own graves, and the opportunity must therefore be taken quickly.

The democrats believe that colonialism in Africa has fulfilled its role, and that the white man, by his presence, contributed to the awakening of the Africans who are now ready to take over. They even understand that the use of anti-white racialism in Africa as a revolutionary weapon was inevitable. Most of them could afford to leave Africa

themselves. But they are in a moral dilemma: by so doing they abandon the white African communities to their fate. Since the profits of
colonial exploitation mostly accrue to European and American interests,
they feel that European liberals, in their enthusiasm and sympathy for
African emancipation, should no longer turn a blind eye to the problems of those who are prepared to let history follow its course. Some
humanitarian interest should now be taken in this subsidiary cause of
anti-colonialism, otherwise a situation will be reached whereby the
prosperous fathers who sent their less conscious children to steal get
away with the additional crime of abandoning them to the fury of the
robbed.

At the time of the 1958 elections, Mozambique democrats were not
so naïve as to believe that General Delgado would be allowed to
become President. On the contrary, they sent an envoy to Brazil and
Portugal to help plan General Delgado's escape to Sao Paulo, prior to
the preparation of an anti-constitutional coup based in a Portuguese
African territory. This, it was hoped, would be turned into the centre
of a Portuguese democratic revolutionary movement. The envoy
was arrested on his return, but Mozambique democrats went on with
other plans and have recently addressed a "Document to the Portuguese President". Dated the 6th April, 1961, this paper, after subtly
recalling how only the manipulation of vote counting had prevented
General Delgado from winning the elections in Mozambique, stated
quite bluntly: "As we see our brothers in Angola paying with their
lives the price of their illusions . . . we want to stress that we face
Mozambique's problems with realism . . . Of the six million of our
population less than one hundred thousand are non-African. . . . As
we see what the dominant powers responsible for the destinies of the
world think about the future of southern Africa . . . we are not prepared to give the Estado Novo a blank cheque on which our future
and that of our children would be compromised . . ."

Looking wistfully north to Tanganyika, where transition to African
emancipation took place without any serious conflict, Mozambique
whites are as worried over the furious tide of black nationalism as they
are about the potential political and diplomatic intrigues of white
extremists in South Africa and the Rhodesias. The demands with which
the document just quoted continued can be summed up as a positive
and realistic approach to the situation. They were:

1. Immediate abolition of the *indigenato* system (Native Statute) and the extension of citizenship rights to every African.

2. A conference of representatives of all sectors of the population, irrespective of race or creed, for the drafting of a Mozambique Statute of Financial and Administrative Autonomy.

3. The Conference to be held in the presence of Portuguese as well as foreign observers and journalists from Europe, the United States, Africa and Asian countries.

4. A guarantee that a Portuguese army force would be posted along the border to prevent foreign intervention.

The Mozambique democrats hope that, in a world riddled with ideological suspicion, their efforts will not be taken as sheer expedient. It is true that Africans would be left in an extremely backward situation, with a literacy rate of less than one per cent—but it is common knowledge that educated Africans, some living in the United States and Europe or organized in Tanganyika, are willing to take over the government by peaceful means. Moreover, the whites realize that Mozambique is not a white man's country, if there is any such country in Africa. Its strategic position in the southern continent, especially if the democratic programme finds the support of Mr. Julius Nyerere as well as that of Rhodesian and South African moderates, could well become crucial in the political trends of the area. Mr. Nyerere's revolution without revenge is by far the most advanced and realistic outlook in the African scene; on the other hand, from a military point of view, Europeans form a very strong political force in this part of Africa and a further expansion of African revolutionary extremism, supported and infiltrated as it is by Soviet political interests, might well bring about a change of heart in the West, favouring the creation of a Formosa-like citadel against black nationalism.

In the desperation of their self-defence, as violent and legitimate as the fury of African extremism, Europeans could still drag the unhappy continent into further misery and loss of human lives, but by a process of peaceful change the white communities could fulfil a useful role in the immediate future of emancipated Africa. The raising of African standards of living and the introduction of high-ranking Africans into local government would promote a revolution in the racial concepts of the white communities and release existing racial tension. In time, by the gradual process of ethnic assimilation to a point that can hardly be visualized now, it is to be hoped that these white communities would be absorbed into the African race or carry on with their lives as naturally as Africans who have settled in Europe.

Barring the adoption of some such solution, the Portuguese Government will continue to augment the white population of Mozambique against all the trends of African politics. Economic expansion cannot cope with unrestricted immigration—unless the Administration maintains its rule of oppression and exploitation, while Africans accumulate justified resentments and grievances against the resident Europeans. In order to avoid blunt apartheid in law, if no change of heart takes place the barrage of lies and sophisms will go on exhausting the imagination of writers and confusing the minds of readers. When the twin black and white sleepers awake and shake off their cocoons there will hardly be time in the ensuing holocaust for them to reflect that the black peoples, turned into rebels, and the whites, turned into reactionaries, were alike the victims of the over-all drama of colonialism that is already reaching a climax in the sister territory of Angola.

CHAPTER IX

ANGOLA

Brazil in Reverse

THERE WERE TWO visions, two histories of Angola—one was written in Portuguese text-books, the other was written in the hearts of Africans. For the Portuguese, Angola was the size they wished their country to be and their hope was to make of Angola a country wherein the two races would eventually be fused and form a new and bigger Portugal. While in the hills of Portugal school teachers proudly showed children the map of Angola superimposed on the map of Europe, to illustrate the Estado Novo's slogan that "Portugal is not a small country", African mothers in the kraals of Angola were teaching their children the more realistic facts about the Portuguese intruders, the descendants of ancient slavers who robbed their soil of its riches and enslaved them anew. It had all begun centuries ago—but in modern times the Estado Novo, in silencing the Portuguese, made any progressive intercourse between the two peoples impossible and led both sides into tragedy.

The ideals of Portuguese colonial policy were traditionally based on the concept of racial equality. This distinctive Portuguese outlook towards race relations derives in part from the realization that the Portuguese themselves are not a pure European race and partly from the contact of centuries with peoples of different races throughout the Empire. Since racial prejudice is essentially an extension of social and economic prejudice and the standards of living and education of the Portuguese lower classes are not much above those of urbanized Africans, the majority of Portuguese are naturally exempt from it. The tenor of traditional thought on the subject is also influenced by Portugal's social and cultural connections with Brazil, a Portuguese-speaking, racial democracy where, in spite of a very mixed population, no serious antagonisms are to be found and the Portuguese element has been the main factor in miscegenation. Theories of ethnic assimilation and the solution of Africa's racial problems through large-scale inter-marriage are therefore not uncommon amongst Portuguese. Furthermore, unlike South Africans, with their Dutch Reformed Church, the overwhelming majority (ninety-five per cent) of Portuguese are at least nominally Catholics and the universalist concepts of the Roman Catholic Church, with its policy of expansion, do not in principle admit of racial discrimination.

In practice, race relations in Portuguese African territories are influenced by a number of local factors and can be said to follow roughly the same pattern of empiricism as the British territories with a similar geographical situation. Race relations in Portuguese East Africa differ from those of Portuguese West Africa as race relations in Kenya differ from those in Ghana. Mozambique is more given to the habits of racial aristocracy than Angola and Portuguese Guinea, where some generations ago the Governor-General was an African. However, even so, the expression of these influences in Portuguese Africa was, until recently, nowhere so intense as to invalidate the marked contrast between race relations in Portuguese territories and those of neighbouring British territories and South Africa. Moreover, the influence of Brazil (the home of many Portuguese), Angola, the Cape Verde islands and Guinea, projected into Portuguese culture in the ramifications of family and social connections throughout the length and breath of Portugal, must render any isolated exception, such as that of Mozambique, comparatively negligible in assessing the general truism.

It was the non-racial ideology that formed the background of the cherished hope of the Portuguese that they could retain Angola under their cultural influence. The Portuguese never really believed that Angola, fourteen times the size of Portugal, could be kept indefinitely under Lisbon rule. Until the rise of African nationalism the hope was that Portugal would succeed in creating in Angola a second Brazil —a Portuguese-speaking, autonomous Republic where the minority white group would dominate by superiority not of race or colour, but of education and social standards.

White separatist movements in Angola can be traced as far back as the nineteenth century. In the late twenties, General Norton de Matos, then Governor-General of Angola, was one of those who supported the demands for Angolan autonomy. At the time, white separatism met with the approval of liberals, and would surely have been regarded as a step forward by a world public opinion on which the views of coloured people had hardly any influence. Under the Republic, Portuguese colonial policy was, for its time, as advanced as that of the other colonial powers. Legislation framed at home was subject, as in other colonial systems, to less liberal application in far away territories, but the Republican Governors often took a firm stand on the issue of the social exploitation of African populations. Furthermore, the Republican regime was responsible for an economic development in these areas which compares favourably with that of the Estado Novo, in spite of its shorter term of office. Indeed most railways, roads and schools in Angola and Mozambique were opened up before the Estado Novo came to power. In the 1920's, Africans from Portuguese territories had their own *Liga Africana* (African League), whose leaders acted as spokesmen for the rights and interests of Africans, on a consultative level. They were among the main forces behind the organization of a Pan-African Conference held in Lisbon in 1923, which was attended by a number of American negro leaders: but, as Portuguese territories seemed to be the constant target of imperialist ambitions on the part of other European powers, a policy of understanding between Portuguese, African and other negro people was deliberately pursued in order to strengthen the Portuguese position in Africa. Dr. Salazar's rise to power was in fact partly determined by a Right-wing fear that prevailing liberal tendencies would lead to the autonomy of Portuguese territories. The totalitarian framework of the regime put a curb on such tendencies among Angolan settlers, but the question of autonomy remained one of the suppressed issues of Portuguese politics.

There are a number of obvious economic and political reasons why Angolan settlers should prefer to go their own way. Angola, like Mozambique, is subject to a central policy whereby its economic development has been greatly hampered by the interests of Portugal itself. Instead of being allowed to industrialize its own resources, economic activity is still essentially confined to the export of a variety of agricultural, tropical and sub-tropical products, such as coffee (some fifty per cent of the total), fish products, sisal, corn and sugar, which are dependent on weather conditions and vulnerable to fluctuations in demand and quotations in the world market. Diamonds are exported to Portugal in raw form. Non-Angolan exploitation of the newly discovered oil deposits near Luanda is seen as yet another example of the exclusion of local capital from the development of the country's resources. The establishment of industries to meet local requirements is conditioned to non-competition with Metropolitan industry. The "one nation" principle has been turned into a potent expedient for the benefit of the party's influential business men, since Metropolitan import firms are allowed to bid for participation in major development projects, or as suppliers of machinery and equipment, much to the detriment of trade interests on the spot. Furthermore, Portugal in fact only buys twenty per cent of Angolan exports and her market capacity for such commodites as coffee (which is mostly sold to the United States) seems to Angolans to offer far too little scope to justify their continued dependence on Portuguese economic rule. A substantial part of Angola's foreign currency earnings, resulting from the surplus in her balance of trade (for, with the exception of the British-owned Benguela Railways which extend to Katanga, Angola has no major sources of income from either services or tourism) is absorbed by her financial commitments to Portugal. The relatively large-scale expenditure on shipping and official tourism to Europe is given priority in these payments. The result is that there is often no currency available to pay for the increasing rate of imports, and Metropolitan exporters have to wait long periods for payment transfers from Angola; meanwhile the senders meet with increased banking transfer premiums, which are tantamount to a devaluation of the Angolan escudo, officially at a par with that of Metropolitan Portugal.

Apart from general grievances against the totalitarian nature of the regime, Angola has a number of political reasons for discontent. Even within the framework of existing institutions, Angola is deprived of any effective representation of its interests in Portugal. At the National Assembly, for instance, representation in these crucial years of political change has been limited to three deputies, whose election is not free and who do not even have to be permanent residents in the territory. Since the Assembly comprises 120 deputies, Angola has evidently been represented far below its economic and political importance. Furthermore, unlike Republican and Monarchist Governments which appointed as High Commissioners and Governors General some of the notable Portuguese politicians of their time, Dr. Salazar has deliberately nominated a number of Navy and Army captains of lesser importance in the Portuguese political scene. Apart also from these purely domestic considerations, Angolan settlers have long realized that the colonial rule of Portugal over Angola left the political future of the country open to uncertainty. Dr. Salazar's regime may have the power to enforce its autocratic constitution internally, but it has been evident over the past few years that United Nations pressure on the question of the Portuguese Empire implies non-acceptance of the "one nation" theory—a legal expedient which never really convinced anyone except those who invented and enforced it. These European settlers regard Angola exactly as a European regards his own country. Some of them have Angola-born grandparents or are related to half-castes. For these people Angola is "the nation"—a nation subjected to Portugal and striving for independence.

The relatively large half-caste element of the civilized Angolan population (some 25,000 people as compared with 80,000 Europeans in 1950) and a number of culturally assimilated Africans have also come to dream of a multi-racial Republic, on the lines of Brazil just across the ocean from Angola. For these people it seemed that once Angola became independent it would forge ahead with remarkable speed. Since the density of the population was one of the lowest in the continent—1·8 per square mile—it would then be possible to accommodate a greater number of Portuguese immigrants while at the same time raising the social standards of Africans. As in the case of Brazil, Portuguese immigrants would be fitted into their non-racial plan.

Ground-floor Occupation

In Angola, unlike Mozambique, the process of social co-existence at the lower strata of society has been officially allowed. Prejudiced foreigners often saw the situation in the deprecating terms of the following passage: "It [Luanda] was Portugal but fused into Africa. Natives and half-castes sat at the wine shops, too, and children of every grade from black to white played in the streets. It was often difficult to distinguish which of the population were Europeans and which African . . . Europe at its lowest standard of living is not far removed from Africa. The Portuguese peasant does not live so differently from the African peasant. The African makes an implicit caste distinction between the big white and the small white; he refers to the Portuguese as the black man of Europe and reacts to him as an equal. Nor to the Portuguese is he essentially inferior. Thus the two races have absorbed one another quite comfortably. I have seen them at school, in hospital and in prison together. They have the same rights, the same judicial system and . . . the same language".[1]

This social phenomenon has nothing metaphysical about it—although it has been the theme of endless academic discussions on the "Portuguese soul". It is a positive trait of Portuguese culture, deriving from a conjunction of negative social factors—and it would be the necessary element in the making of a new "Brazil". Furthermore, a stage had been reached in Angola whereby the population preferred Brazilian literature and manufactures to those of Portugal and looked wistfully to the democratic patterns of Brazilian life.

Dr. Salazar's own policies, in their insane, ultra-nationalist dream, aimed, on the contrary, at keeping Angola as free from non-Portuguese influence as possible—in point of fact he is accused by none other than the Brazilian Ambassador, Mr. Alvaro Lins, of systematically opposing the influence of Brazil in Angola. The policy of increasing the settlement of Portuguese in Angola became a manner of counter-balancing separatist tendencies by the introduction of large numbers of fresh and more reliable immigrants. This policy faced a number of difficulties, as the rate of economic expansion was hardly adequate to accommodate such an increase in the European population, but luckily the impoverished Portuguese peasants were not particularly demanding in the matter of living standards, and it would take them a long time to understand the issues of separatism. Furthermore, they would form an occupation force in the event of a threat from African nationalism, and it was hoped that a social situation would be created whereby the division of class and race would in time be confused—not as a consequence of any considerable number of Africans having infiltrated the ranks of the predominantly European upper classes, but by the fact that the poor white element would become absorbed in the African proletariat.

The massive settlement schemes on which the Estado Novo embarked closely resembled those carried out by Fascist Italy in her East African Empire of the 1930's. Under these "Land Settlement Schemes", which were an important part of consecutive Six Year Development plans, large areas were prepared in Angola by means of agricultural hydraulic development, irrigation and drainage. Entire villages similar to those of the Portuguese countryside were built. The *Colonos*, their

[1] J. Patrick Balfour, *Lords of the Equator: An African Journey*, Hutchinson, London, 1937.

travelling expenses paid by the Government, were given land and tools. Under these schemes, thousands of families have been settled in Angola over the past few years, but this poor substitute for a Portuguese agrarian reform was no dynamic new ideal. Its slogan, "A hoe to each man", recalled the archaic standards of Portuguese agriculture. Nor is it particularly rewarding to anyone. The meagre incomes of the *colonos*, in the £200 a year range, are substantially reduced by the repayment of travelling and settling expenses to the Estado. The debt keeps them imprisoned in the settlement. The great distances in Africa put travel beyond their means and, remembering with inarticulate sadness the villages and fields of Portugal, the settlers often complain of having gained less than they lost. Unaware of the niceties of African politics, they would go back if only they could—but the Government takes care to bring their families too, and return fares are not foreseen in the plan.

The relaxation of immigration formalities extended the rush to settle Portuguese in Angola to practically anybody who could afford to travel and wanted to settle on his own initiative. As a result of these policies the number of white settlers rose progressively from 44,000 in 1940 to 78,000 in 1950 and 110,000 in 1955. From 1955 to 1960 the population rose spectacularly by 90,000 to 200,000 people and new social problems were created. Not only were Africans denied the few opportunities that inadequate economic expansion offered, but in some cases they were replaced by the poor whites. Many an illiterate Portuguese peasant has joined the ranks of Angolan illiterates (who in 1950, accounted for over ninety-nine per cent of the African population and approximately twenty-five per cent of the Europeans). Literate Africans often write letters on behalf of illiterate white peasants to their relatives at home, and until recently racial antagonism scarcely existed at any level of their social intercourse. Unemployment became a problem amongst whites as well as among half-castes and educated Africans. In Angola there are indeed blacks with higher incomes than whites, and the phenomenon of a division of the general population by class rather than race was embryonic.

The Tragic Awakening

Meanwhile, in the upper strata of society, where men and women keep strictly to their own circles, business was going on as usual;

the Bank of Angola, the Companhia dos Diamantes de Angola, Comgeral Purifina, the Sociedade Agricola do Cassequel, for instance, were making net profits which average forty-nine per cent of their capital. Under the ideals of the "one nation" and the cloak of censorship no one could do more than whisper a criticism based on facts within the range of his own daily experience. The oppressive rule of Dr. Salazar seemed as unchallengeable in Angola as anywhere in the sleeping Empire.

But the calm was deceptive, such was the importance of the Angolan issue to Portuguese democrats that General Norton de Matos had been chosen as democratic candidate in 1949 because, among other reasons, he would reopen the issue of Angolan antonomy, the dream that was the main cause of his dismissal by the Estado Novo right at the outset of its establishment. In 1947, when most modern African leaders were still at school, another Portuguese democrat, Henrique Galvao, conceived the idea of relieving Angolans from the rigours of the feudal colonialism imposed by the Estado Novo in a report that surpasses in vehemence anything that has since been written on the subject. Since then Angola has indeed been the background to his whole political career as an apostate of Dr. Salazar's regime—a career which stands as witness to the bitter history of Portuguese liberalism under the present regime: first in his fierce sixteen-year sentence, then, in 1961, in his escape to make his desperate mid-ocean cry for freedom.

Had Galvao reached Angola in the *Santa Maria* the revolutionary trend might have followed its just course: the guns might have been directed towards the real oppressors. There were other liberals awaiting him in Angola, for the Portuguese were being told of appalling repressions being committed there since 1959 in an attempt to crush a revolutionary movement towards African self-assertion. Africans were being shot and tortured and Portuguese liberals themselves were being arrested and refused fair trials.

The Luanda risings that followed the surrender of the *Santa Maria* were essentially ideological and non-racial. White Portuguese nationals, as well as coloured people, sided with the African rebels in a suicidal attack as desperate in its fashion as the Caribbean piracy. The Portuguese wanted the chance to review their problems and to accept with dignity the transition to African self-government. Nor would it have been the first time that Portuguese had fought among themselves to attain the emancipation of a former colony: it was a Portuguese who shouted "Independence or death" and led Brazil to freedom. But the Estado Novo had brought the possibilities of opposition so low that Portuguese democrats could only meet with pathetic frustration in their little floating battle for a free nation. Instead, the separatist issue was overtaken by the tide of African nationalism. The Estado Novo, and Portugal with it, were caught by the more brutal forces of an ultra-modern revolution.

So modern was this revolution when it came that it used the hysterical fury of the African tribes to wage a genocidal war, apparently studied to provoke the no less appalling fury of Fascist forces of the other side against millions of African hostages who were caught in the ensuing bloodbath. Once the spark of racial hatred had caught hold, all possibility of collaboration and understanding were for the moment wiped out from the face of Angola; though, alas, not even the racial divisions are conclusive, for in spite of their common grievances against the white man Africans are yet divided and sub-divided amongst themselves by tribal and ideological differences.

The One Nation versus Black Nationalism

The history of the modern revolutionary process in Angola will never be accurately written—most of it is hidden in administrative and Police records and not everything is even written there. Much of it was planned abroad, in Leopoldville, the headquarters of the *Uniao das Populacoes de Angola* (Union of the Peoples of Angola, or UPA), and at Conakry and Accra, where the *Movimento Popular de Libertacao de Angola* (Peoples Movement for the Liberation of Angola, or MPLA) has been based. These conspirators were beyond the range of the Portuguese PIDE, which explains their comparatively high degree of organization. Their two movements came to represent the two major political currents in the tide of Angolan revolution, which has been creeping in for years but was kept out of the news by Dr. Salazar's censors until it was no longer possible to hide it.

The MPLA is the better known party to the Portuguese, and is easier to identify; some of its leaders, such as Ilidio Machado and Dr. Agostinho Neto are now in prison in Cape Verde, and the latter was formerly the cell-mate of Portuguese democrats when he lived in Portugal. Others, such as the gifted poet Mario de Andrade, the acting President, are well known to Portuguese intellectuals. Some are the husbands of Portuguese women. The political thought of the

5—PAIE

Portuguese opposition, being well to the Left, can be said to have been the first influence in the political conceptions of these African leaders. Furthermore, Portuguese-educated Africans share the vision of Angola as a national entity, and their political ideology in this respect can be defined as the African equivalent of white separatism. Their version foresees an independent African socialist state where Africans would not be unduly disturbed by the continued presence of white Portuguese socialists in their sparsely populated country. The MPLA having enjoyed the support of Portuguese democrats in Angola itself, the Portuguese still trust that, in the long run, ideologic affinities must be stronger than temporary divisions on the national plane. Indeed, many Portuguese democrats in Angola hoped that a movement for African emancipation having been successful, the struggle would be continued, as in the case of Brazil, by a democratic war waged on the Portuguese in their own country. The aims of the UPA are a little more ambiguous. Its leader, Roberto Holden, is better known in America, where he was received by President Kennedy on 25th April, 1961, than he is in Portugal, and he does not see eye to eye with the MPLA. The UPA started operating some five years ago in the Belgian Congo as the Union of the Peoples of Northern Angola. In fact most of its supporters were Bakongo, a powerful tribe inhabiting the lower areas of the former French and Belgian Congos as well as Angola's northernmost region, also named Distrito do Congo. Apparently Mr. Roberto Holden does not like the Portuguese and all his propaganda slogans seem to be of the type that refers to the Portuguese as the black man of Africa (a phrase uncomplimentary to Africans themselves if used in a pejorative way). The UPA is also known to have had the sympathies of Mr. Kasavubu who, like the Abbé Youlou, President of the former French Congo, dreamt of a resurgence of the Bakongo kingdom from which the Abako movement sprang.

The Portuguese have been for so long in Angola that they too might almost be considered an African tribe. This area and the Bakongo people are well known to them. Centuries ago they enjoyed amicable relations with the king and his subjects—some of whom were partners in the lucrative business of the slave trade, in which, incidentally, the supply actually exceeded demand. But Portugal is too small a country to cope with revolutions which are planned as far away as Leopoldville, if not farther. The State Police are only accustomed to putting down minor local rebellions, whereas

over the past few years they have found themselves outnumbered in
Angola by one to a thousand. With hundreds of thousands of emigrants
settled just across the border of the Congo, the ideals of African self-
assertion have spread to Angloa like an infection, though the parochial
colonialism of the Estado Novo has, in many ways, for long put a
brake on its progress. For all their illusory and outdated aspects, inter-
race relations in Portuguese Africa, as we have seen, were until recently
almost free of the more evident forms of hatred that prevail in South
Africa and the Rhodesias. White, black and half-caste children went to
school together, and if discrimination was practised in many hypo-
critical ways, there were enough inter-marriages to invalidate the
sense of social division on a racial basis. Indeed, in the Army, the
soldiers were mostly Africans; the PIDE in Angola has black employees
as agents spying indiscriminately on blacks as well as whites, and
Portuguese progressives conspire together with Africans. This situation
has been a hindrance to the extremists, for it does not meet with the
prerequisites of their text-books which proclaim the principle that
the race issue is the only revolutionary force accessible to the African
masses, especially since they are mostly illiterate and could hardly be
taught political theories anyway. According to this school of revolutionary thought, therefore, white liberalism is unwelcome in Africa
as a clouding of the issue, useful only in Europe and the United States
where a good Press is a necessary element of revolutionary tactics.
"When we cut the white men's throats we won't look at their faces,"
say the more arrogant African rebels everywhere by way of explaining
the exclusion of white humanitarians from their midst. Although the
whites of Europe and America, more concerned with interplanetary
travel than with Africa, may be able to afford to look upon such
remarks with contempt, the tiny minority of white employees of
European and American concerns in Southern Africa have every reason
to be increasingly worried.

Over the past few years, especially in the northern half of Angola,
the situation has changed: even second generation *assimilados* have
shown a growing tendency to return to their African condition.
African women have been replacing their European-style outfits by
the traditional robes of their people. Africans in general have become
more and more interested in re-learning tribal languages and there
has been a widespread re-identification with indigenous culture.
Suddenly Africans were no longer looking West, across the ocean

to Brazil. Their eyes were turned North, to the resurgence of African nationalism. This legitimate cultural awakening of an African conscience was not necessarily instigated by supposed political agents, although it provided the right ground for their activities and they are known to have been operating in Portuguese Africa both at urban and tribal levels. In the overwhelming majority of cases it reflected a spontaneous tendency towards self-assertion.

By 1961 the atmosphere had become heavily charged. Alarming rumours of appalling repressive measures on the part of the Portuguese Police were obviously not totally unfounded—though some widely credited stories of such things as the distribution of poisoned food to stores for sale to the African public, or the dropping of African leaders from planes into the bottom of the sea, may seem too dangerous, too indiscreet and too expensive for Portuguese repressive standards! The frightening stories of African risings and atrocities spread simultaneously amongst the Europeans themselves did not always correspond to fact either, and were part of a psychological process of cause and effect which did much to undermine European morale. But Africans could no longer be trusted. Even the Lisbon-born Vicar-General of Angola, Manuel das Neves, whom the Portuguese nationalist Press described as "suave mannered and respected" had turned out to be a rebel leader and thereby earned the epithet of "Judas" (for nationalists have always identified their causes with those of God).

There are other events which cannot be easily explained, perhaps even by those who took part in them, but the programme of guerrilla-type terrorist warfare that broke out in Northern Angola fits into a pattern of extremist tactics. Admittedly the Africans, without modern weapons (which in any case they would be technically unable to operate), have to improvise their own methods of attack adapted to African conditions; yet not only do assaults on isolated stores, administrative outputs and European villages that are no more than trading centres prove to be an effective way of causing economic disruption, but the character of atrocities committed on Europeans, ranging from rape and mutilation of women and children to putting out people's eyes, skinning alive and severing the sexual organs of little boys, is a sort of home-made African atomic weapon that has devastating psychological consequences among the white population scattered throughout areas the size of European countries. It would, in fact, be deliberate blindness to dismiss such practices as the mere spontaneous expression of hatred released. For one thing, the UPA leaders have been financed internationally, and they announced in December 1960, at carefully prepared Press conferences and meetings, that they would launch an offensive. For another, these leaders had every reason to know that whites would be provoked into massive emotional retaliation against millions of defenceless Africans who would be the hostages of race hatred. The claim of Roberto Holden, reported in the American Press, that the rebels had only been instructed to practise sabotage, but had got out of hand, seems like an echo of the Belgian Congo situation.

The international scale of the Angolan conflict can be judged by the United Nations' reaction. Soon, as was to be expected, little forgotten Portugal had the honour of attracting the critical attention of practically every delegate, especially the Russian delegate, who called the Angola situation "a shameful phenomenon which must be eliminated"—a verdict which closely resembles that of Portuguese democrats on the Angola issue, as well as on the handling of the Hungarian uprisings. With the Soviets once again patronizing the cause of freedom of a people who are not under their domination, Portuguese humanitarians began to be worried lest Angolan Africans be led into a situation whereby the centuries-old system of forced labour would not even now be finally abolished. The chorus of criticism at the United Nations came from every side, however, until the only complimentary interventions were those of the Portuguese delgate himself.

Meanwhile, in the short space of two months Angola, where the Portuguese have been established for hundreds of years, had come to feel to Africans like an occupied country. Race relations had passed from the paternalistic and accommodating phase into that of a reciprocal genocidal war. Over one thousand Europeans and thirty thousand Africans had been brutally slaughtered. The Africans, their faces painted red, excited by tribal ceremonies, were nevertheless usually careful enough to ensure that able-bodied men had been attracted away from the scene of attack, leaving women and children behind. The shouts of "Lumumba" by the UPA rebels, evoking a revenge for the many martyrs of African emancipation, were only exceeded in hatred by the shouts of "Kill them all" from enraged Europeans, who resorted to lynchings as alien to their nature as violence is to the average African. This land where Africans had come to know peace, though never right and justice, was suddenly the scene of a legend of horror. The Portuguese Army, under the command of the most rabid of the Fascist wing, engaged in an emotional campaign of retaliation, releasing on defenceless peoples the fury of their exalted ultra-nationalism, the frustration of political errors, the disappointment of what they conceived to be the betrayal of their ideological allies. There are no accurate accounts of the number of dead. Unused to this type of warfare, Portuguese soldiers in areas known to be occupied by rebels ruthlessly eliminated every African they spotted. They simplified matters by dropping napalm bombs, causing the devastation of small-scale Hiroshimas. Entire villages were destroyed. Houses in which Africans were sheltering were strafed and fleeing men, women and children machine-gunned in open fields. Troops went forth from village to village burning huts and slaying the innocent at random. These horrors were matched in Lisbon by the cold-blooded attitude of the nationalist and Catholic Press briefing the departing soldiers for the war. The "mopping up operations" that were announced suggested the extermination of the rebels like vermin. The Fascists are determined on a bloodbath for Africans who dare to oppose their rule. All in all it is another unworthy page in the history of the twentieth century.

Repercussions

The crisis reached such proportions that Angola, five times the size of the United Kingdom, had to be covered with a still more rigid curtain of censorship, which now openly extended to correspondence. The Portuguese Minister for Overseas Affairs, Professor Adriano Moreira, known as a prominent member of the Portuguese United Nations delegation, set up headquarters in Angola. The richer Europeans sent their wives and children home and only stopped going themselves when Dr. Salazar passed a law prohibiting all males between the ages of eighteen and forty-five from leaving Angola. The Army appealed to settlers to "show your gratitude: to leave now is treason", and took special measures to get the coffee crop harvested by Africans under their protection.

The only conventional feature of the Angola conflict was the fact that on both sides the promoters kept conveniently hundreds, if not thousands, of miles away from the scene of battle, while illiterate Africans, unaware of the sophisticated theories and doctrines of politicians, slaughtered the underpaid white tradesmen of the area, who are no more than the agents of colonialist and commercial interests in Europe.

The repercussions of the Angola tragedy were soon felt throughout the white-dominated sub-continent. In some respects the moral impact was even greater than that of the Congo, for the Belgians had never quite been regarded as white Africans. Even the crises in Kenya and Algeria can be regarded as isolated phenomena with little psychological significance in comparison with the Angolan war. In the Rhodesias, South Africa, South West Africa and Mozambique increased precautions were taken to prevent surprise attack. An internal *coup d'état* was aborted in Lisbon, with the result that Dr. Salazar himself assumed the command of Portuguese troops. He divided his energies between a routine of meetings with the General Staff and devout reflections and prayers. In both these routine procedures he found the inspiration to send an avenging force estimated at 25,000 Portuguese troops to Angola, which, together with those already stationed there and the mobilization of local territorials, make up some twenty-five per cent of the total existing white population.

His solution is only exceeded in idealistic inspiration by the contents of the programme published on the other side by the leaders of the African Liberation Movement, which at this stage has a united front. According to their manifesto, which justly aims at "getting rid of the colonialists and achieving the immediate and complete independence of the Angolan homeland", Africans have declared war on the Portuguese in the Algerian fashion. In the event of its success, Portuguese and other foreigners are to be deprived of all the advantages they have enjoyed under the colonial system; the privileges of Portuguese and other foreign companies are to be ended (although foreign concerns which conform to the new laws will be protected). Without mention of any large-scale foreign aid, which would be essential to an over-all economic readjustment, forced labour, the basis of the Angolan economy, is to be summarily abolished while exports are to be stepped up; the State apparatus is to be Africanized, although Africans are the first to realize that only 0·7 per cent of Angolans are literate, and little more than twenty have so far graduated at universities. At the same time, the programme gives friendly warning that this new, free Angolan Government would review Angola's position in relation to the foreign treaties, agreements and alliances to which Portugal has committed her, and contains a veiled threat that all traitors and enemies of the Angolan Republic-to-be will suffer confiscation of their land. Furthermore, each nationality or ethnic group is to have the right to use and develop its own language, create its own script and preserve and renew its cultural heritage. To sum up, it is nearly as idealistic and ambitious a project as Dr. Salazar's dream of the "one nation", for it seems that, where Dr. Salazar wanted to give too little, the Africans are demanding too much too soon.

The political situation in Portugal itself also gave cause for anxiety. The nature of the Estado Novo as a Fascist regime was partly responsible for the sympathy Africans met with in the influential liberal Press throughout the democratic world. Deserted by one and all, Dr. Salazar turned to Franco to emphasize the ideological character of the Angola conflict—the new "crusade" for which their extremist armies had been waiting. Meanwhile, Portugal having announced its obstinacy in defending Africa, the Western diplomats, their minds at peace, went on supporting the African cause. It never even occurred to the Estado Novo, deprived of many of the best Portuguese brains, that, in view of the tremendous international implications of the situation, the only way to get support might rather be to announce a readiness to pursue a policy of evacuation and abandonment!

The political and economic consequences of the crisis were decisive. Even Dr. Salazar himself, a man never willing to concede defeat, concluded that, in the field of race relations, "the work of centuries had been destroyed in a month". Whatever the outcome, the reconciliation of the Africans and the Portuguese would prove to be a tremendous and slow task, made the more difficult for the friction that would continue to be fed from outside. Angola, with a budget hardly exceeding £25 million, could not cope with the increasing expenditure on military efforts, especially at a time when her revenues were likely to decrease as a consequence of the economic disruption caused by the guerrilla war. Angola's national debt soon soared to figures out of all proportion to her balance-sheet. The Portuguese themselves awoke to the consequences of Dr. Salazar's colonial policies. Colonialism had long been dead throughout most of Africa, and many problems of transition had elsewhere been solved with intelligence and common sense. They saw Dr. Salazar making reforms far too late in the day and finally commenting "perhaps I have lived beyond my time". In spite of this, Dr. Salazar was still able to drag with him a new contingent of younger nationalists who devoted their efforts to trying to see their way clear out of the mess their leader had created.

Angola is indeed the battlefield of a new war—the scene of a complex political phenomenon which is perhaps even more complicated than that of the Congo itself, which is saying something. Essentially it is the struggle between the Portuguese who believe that their country—the Empire lost—is doomed to extinction, on the one hand, and the Africans engaged in a desperate fight for the birth of their own Angola on the other.

It may also prove to be the first actual battlefield of Portuguese ideological conflicts. Portuguese democrats have no reason to like the UPA, but they do not side with the Estado Novo against the MPLA. They believe that for the UPA to exhort the name of Lumumba is misappropriation, for, after all, Lumumba was handed over to Tshombe by the Bakongo and has only become their martyr after being conveniently buried. But the Lumumbas of Angola are Ilidio Machado, Agostinho Neto, Mario de Andrade, and these people know that the cause of Portuguese democracy is intertwined with their own. It is possible that if Dr. Salazar were to succeed in curbing the Angolan revolution the Portuguese democratic movements abroad would side with the MPLA to carry on with the common struggle. In his determination to keep Angola, Dr. Salazar is relieving Portugal of most of its Fascist troops, and he will not be able to cope with any rebellious situation in Portugal itself. Furthermore, he is now forced to wage a war on his sacred budget, and the possibility is that, if the Angola conflict lasts too long, the national budget will revert to the disastrous condition in which he found it. The expected emergency increases in taxation, the economic, political and moral implications of the "Angola adventure"—as it is bitterly called amongst Portuguese democrats—may well prove to be the end of the dictator.

Inside the curtain officially clamped over Angola Portuguese colonialism is dying before the eyes of 4,500,000 black and 200,000 white Africans. It will never be the same again. A new nation is being born in pain.

Chapter X

SALAZAR'S DAY OF RECKONING

Portugal without Friends

THE PROCESS OF disintegration of the last Portuguese Empire having begun, not for the first time in its history Portugal finds itself dramatically absorbed with its overseas problems. The combination of colonialism and dictatorship has created a unique and complex phenomenon in the modern world. The "one nation" has not been under Parliamentary government and the rule of the Censor and the Police has kept the Portuguese people in complete ignorance of their overseas affairs. For over thirty years the mere suggestion of independence to any Portuguese territory would have been regarded as high treason if it ever succeeded in being published. Dr. Salazar has been quick to seize on the dramatic losses of Portuguese settlers in Angola to stir up nationalist emotions. Rebels are dismissed as Communists or alternatively as drugged tribesmen. The adverse voting at the United Nations, where the Portuguese delegation can now count on the support of only Spain and South Africa, is described as being inspired by Soviet imperialism, Pan-Africanism or covetous crypto-imperialists in the Western world.

Once again, the Portuguese look with apprehension to their economic future and to the loss of the capital and work they have invested in their overseas territories. Although the revolutionary process of the emancipation of colonial peoples is beyond national control, Dr. Salazar's responsibilities are nevertheless exceedingly grave.

Originally the "one nation" constitution and the extension of totalitarian rule to the Empire was inspired by a determination to curb white separatism. Backward and impoverished, Portugal could only impose its colonial exploitation on the vast and dispersed imperial remains by authoritarian rule. If freedom of the Press and Parliamentary government had been allowed it would have been impossible to contain the growing demands of the European settlers in Mozambique and Angola, which were the only considerable political threat to the unity of the Empire. For the success of his policies, Dr. Salazar counted on the triumph of Fascism. In 1936, announcing the aims of his neo-imperialism, he proclaimed: "Economic conditions prevailing in the world today are unlikely to have an adverse affect on the completion of this programme; in fact, it seems to me that the present moment is an exceptionally favourable one for its execution."[1] It was in 1939 that, sharing the Fascist opinion that the future of the British in Southern Africa would not survive the conflict with aggressive Nazism, he sought the diplomatic protection of South Africa, then displaying her own Fascist tendencies. The occasion was the visit of the Portuguese President, General Carmona, to Portuguese colonies and their powerful neighbour. Commenting on the visit, Dr. Salazar made the following remarkably paradoxical statement, which will no doubt provide food for thought among students of the traditional Anglo-Portuguese Alliance:

"We feel . . . that to regard Africa as the commonplace of Europe is no longer in accordance with reality; it may have been so in the past, but it will scarcely be so in the future; and we feel also that for Europe to speak exclusively in the name of Africa likewise belongs to the past. There are interests which it is difficult to discuss in Europe and sovereignties which on the continent of Africa impose themselves with the force and evidence of reality. A vast and prosperous country, forming part of the British Commonwealth, has grown up on the frontier of our colonies in Africa, and between our colonies and that country there exists an understanding, good will and mutual respect which has transformed into fruitful co-operation the rivalry, envy and friction that could only have jeopardized peace and common development."[2]

After the war Dr. Salazar clung fiercely to the protection of the United States, which saw in Portugal, with the islands of the Azores, and its geographical position in the Iberian Peninsula, an important link in the State Department's strategic plans for the Atlantic and the entrance of the Mediterranean. Much of Dr. Salazar's internal prestige derived from these well publicised United States connections, on which the security and support of Portuguese colonialism in

[1] Speech at Economic Conference on Portuguese Empire, June 1936.
[2] Speech at National Assembly, 22.5.39.

Afro-Asian areas depended. While Mr. Dulles pointedly referred to Goa as a Portuguese "province", President Eisenhower himself stated, as recently as May 1960, that "Portugal and the United States have worked together without a single difference of opinion".

Dr. Salazar's persuasive diplomatic argument has always been that the loss of the Portuguese Empire would be followed by such an extensive economic and social crisis in Portugal that the way would be opened to widespread political subversion and Communism. The repercussions of a political reform or revolution in Portugal would obviously upset strategic arrangements in Iberia and would lead to the further weakening of Franco in Spain. While massive economic and financial aid has often rescued Franco from his difficulties, Portugal also obtained a number of substantial loans on behalf of the overseas territories. The military aid systematically supplied to the regime is used as an essential part of the Portuguese repressive machine and is constantly paraded up and down the country, not for the benefit of the non-existent Soviet diplomats, but as a means of intimidating the oppressed people themselves.

Today, however, Dr. Salazar finds himself bereft of international support and tries to transfer responsibility for his own errors by condoning and subtly promoting anti-American demonstrations throughout Portugal and its Empire. In Lisbon, the United States Embassy has been stoned: in Luanda the American consul's car was thrown into the bay; during a bull-fight in Lourenço Marques, thousands of pamphlets claiming "independence for Red Indians" were dropped from the air, and a crowd of ten thousand people, headed by the Mayor, listened to anti-American speeches. The police either turn a blind eye or, disguised as civilians, take an active part in such proceedings. In the process Dr. Salazar is even gaining a certain measure of popular support and the Government is appealing to the people to shed political grievances and to unite in the face of the present emergency.

The crisis, however, is far more catastrophic than Dr. Salazar would like the Portuguese people to believe. The far-flung Portuguese Empire is extremely vulnerable. Portuguese Guinea is not only surrounded by sympathetic members of the French Union but has the independent Republic of Guinea for a neighbour—a territory which has been one of the main anti-Portuguese colonialist centres. Indeed, the Headquarters of the Revolutionary Front for National Independence of Portuguese Colonies is based at Conakry. The African movements of

Mozambique are now established just over the northern border, at Lindi in Tanganyika, where TANU has provided them with a house and funds. Goa, as we have seen, has been the cause of diplomatic dispute as well as non-violent invasions by Goans resident in India. Timor is relatively close to the Independent Republic of Indonesia. A simultaneous armed pressure on all these territories would have a decisive material and moral impact, which would almost inevitably bring about a spectacular disintegration of the Portuguese Empire before the United Nations could possibly untangle the legal complexities of the situation.

The realization of immediate and future problems such as these has led to profound divisions inside the ranks of the regime and the Army itself. The aborted *coup d'état* of April 1961, which involved the former President Craveiro Lopes, the Defence Minister, General Botelho Moniz, and other leading Army Generals, was an expression of these divisions. The essential aim of this faction was to force the resignation of Dr. Salazar, prior to a long overdue revision of Portuguese problems, especially of those pertaining to the overseas territories. Dr. Salazar was saved at the last moment by the powerful ultra-nationalist faction in the Army, built up by Lieutenant-Colonel Santos Costa. Declaring a State of Emergency in Angola, he took iron measures to speed up the arrival of troops on the scene of the terrorist activities, which had reached unforeseen proportions. The Civil Defence (*Defesa Civil do Territorio*) extended its activities to Angola and Mozambique, where a volunteer armed corps had been formed. Throughout Portugal a women's league launched a "Campaign for Gold", aiming at collecting jewellery to aid the Government's efforts in Africa.

In the view of the faction headed by Dr. Salazar, the Portuguese must remain in Africa, not only to save Portuguese lives and capital but to save the West from further dangerous subversion in the southern half of the continent—the *vontade nacional* (national will) does not accept compromise. Those "who even think of negotiation are traitors to their country", so proclaim the extremist journalists who are allowed to cover Angolan events for Portuguese newspapers and news agencies. The legitimate task of protecting the lives of Portuguese people and maintaining public order is confused with a war not only against Black Nationalism and Pan-Africanism, but Bolshevism, Liberalism, Protestantism and the World Press. Communists are invented constantly. Following the traditional extremist tenet that "those who are not for us are against us", humanitarians are called defeatists and doubters dismissed as "demoralizing agents".

Such is the chaos that it does not occur to anyone in this faction that perhaps the terrorist war waged on the Portuguese is a product of African despair in the face of the regime's own "one nation" constitution (which implies the perpetuity of Portuguese rule) and its imperialist and repressive policies.

Democrats meet with the usual rough treatment. In May 1961, under the responsibility of a *Directorio Republicano*, they decided to circulate a 20,000-word programme aiming at the democratization of the Republic. They legitimately asked what could possibly be happening in the Empire to enable close on one hundred thousand armed terrorists to roam around Africa preparing for rebellion unnoticed by the authorities. Once again they demanded, too, the restoration of democracy, liberation of political prisoners, abolition of political courts, censorship and the Secret Police. They avoided the charge of high treason by limiting their proposals for Africa to a demand for severe punishment for racial, political and other discrimination. But once again the sponsors, also supported by the *Seara Nova* (New Crop) group who have aged in their brave and obstinate struggle against the regime, were jailed for investigation.

Conclusions

Since the opponents of Dr. Salazar, in the circumstances of Portuguese life, are only able to express a personal opinion, or that of a comparatively small group of people with whom they can communicate, it is fitting that this book should end as it began by expressing the views of the young men of the author's generation in Portugal and Portuguese Africa, who are entitled to be heard, since, after all, they are the people who will have to cope with the future problems of the country. They are qualified to judge the present situation but are not old enough to have been implicated either in the Republican period or in the establishment and development of the present regime and its policies. Little is known in Portugal itself about the thoughts and opinions of this generation, brought up under police rule, but none the less aware of a tacit internal affinity, whereby the very sons of ministers and police inspectors are often arrested together with the sons of democrats. Their only direct dealings with Portuguese politics so far have been occasional exchanges with the State Police. It is a bitter generation. Dr. Salazar himself has only once interfered with it, and he is unknowingly one of their favourite humorists. In a speech in December 1958 in which he concluded that "the common people only want to be well led and well ruled", he summed up what must have been said to him by the State Police who keep in close touch with him in his ivory governmental tomb: "I have heard tell that some young people today . . . suffer from a kind of anguish, complaining that their souls are empty, and that many of them try to fill this vacuum by absorbing Communist doctrines . . . I fear the intensified materialism that is approaching with all the splendour of its wealth, and the influence it will have on people's souls . . . But . . . why should the young feel that their souls are empty? Are they not sufficiently filled by love of their country, family devotion, the history of their ancestors, beliefs inherited or acquired, aspirations for the future, work, studies . . . ? Something is wrong with our educational work . . ."

There is no "anguish in the souls" of the new generation: only a very justified puzzlement and worry. They may never have read Marx or Lenin, but they can see and judge for themselves the nature of Portuguese society. Wherever they turn they see repression, fear and hypocrisy, from presidents elected in rigged elections down to the police informers who get 30s. to help in the arrest of a man.

The Portuguese of today are confronted with enormous socio-economic problems: among them the structural underdevelopment of their country and the inequalities of its society, the vulnerability of a largely uneducated population to superstitions about economic saviours and well intentioned *coups d'état*, and the implications of a revolutionary emancipation of African territories. Although the conjunction of adverse factors must eventually produce a crisis sufficient to expose the sham of Dr. Salazar's supposedly Messianic genius, and though it might seem politic to allow the full consequences of the disintegration of the Empire to fall squarely on his shoulders, there are responsible young Portuguese ready to undertake the complex task of steering Portugal through this dangerous period in his place, if only on human and Christian grounds, to prevent the tragedy of involving illiterate Portuguese soldiers in armed conflict with equally illiterate rebels.

The claims the democratic opposition have repeatedly made over the last thirty-five years have been confined to such subjects as free elections, revision of electoral rolls and freedom of Press and association.

For this alone a countless number of men and women have been jailed and tortured; others have been dismissed, ruined, separated from their families. As a sample of its civilization, this is the true shame of Portugal. The world knows that Portugal is poor and small—what the world cannot understand is how the minds of the people are directed towards the cult of their ancestors and channelled into a narrowly patriotic nationalism that makes even a people that is itself in subjection appear as the oppressive rulers of other peoples.

To this generation it seems self-evident that Dr. Salazar, as was to be expected, has failed in his attempt to stave off the long overdue social reform in Portugal by means of imperialist expansion in Portuguese Africa. Only national selfishness could blind the ruling Portuguese to the essential problems of the Empire. Into their insane dream of a single nation separated by thousands of miles, inhabited by a diversity of peoples who have their own cultural entities and face their own social and economic problems, the Estado Novo has dragged such causes as Catholicism and Western Democracy. It has also created a new problem, which is the future of thousands of Portuguese families who have settled in Portuguese Angola and Mozambique and who, like Mr. Lumumba, are "in love with the soil of Africa" and look upon it as their home.

To take the Catholic Church first, this has been one of the major victims of Dr. Salazar's bigotry, and for this fact Rome has only to thank the reactionary but powerful faction responsible for Catholic interests in Portugal and Portuguese Africa. It has lived in a state of comprehensible financial dependence on the Estado Novo, but has paid a very high political price for it. Its association with the Estado Novo was one of the factors behind the promulgation of the *Estatuto Missionario* (Missionary Statute) which the regime turned into an instrument of colonialism. With few exceptions, Catholic clerics of all ranks have associated themselves with the insane hypocrisy that denies the self-evident: that in Portuguese Africa the populations are mercilessly exploited and often meet with the most inhuman, let alone unChristian, treatment. The outspoken attitudes of the Bishops of Oporto and Evora, the vibrant and lonely voice of the Bishop of Beira, in Mozambique, and the arrest of the Archbishop of Luanda's secretary in Angola, as well as that of other prominent Catholic ecclesiastics and laymen, have been at best interpreted as a reflection of individual views, at worst as a belated policy of neutrality. The Protestants, though few, seem to take Christianity more seriously.

In spite of its bitter experience with the Republic, when anti-clericalism was rather an expression of anti-Monarchist feeling than anti-religious reaction as such, the Church in Portugal should know better than to associate itself with unpopular regimes of authority. Since political thought is suppressed in Portugal and Portuguese Africa, the only other doctrine that has access to the mass of the people is Communism, which relies for its propagation in Portugal mainly on clandestine Party activities, such as the publication of newspapers: in Africa, trained agents are known to operate amongst tribal and urban populations. The anti-materialistic teachings of Catholicism are thus made to appear as an alternative political creed, but the Church loses in the contrast. For one thing, Communist agents are arrested; for another, the priests have a tendency to associate with the rich and the powerful and, in Africa, they are in any case mostly white and not always exempt from the sin of racial prejudice.

In Portugal there are over 4,200 parishes, thirty seminaries and the Catholic Action Movement claims to have over one hundred thousand members. However, not only are these figures proportionately below those of democratic countries with a predominantly Catholic population, but Portuguese Catholicism, as practised by the majority of Portuguese people, is at best a matter of ancestral routine, at worst a form of pagan superstition. In Portuguese Africa, the civilizing mission proclaimed by the Estado Novo falls incredibly below the standards of other less vocally Catholic countries. While in the continent as a whole there is one African cardinal and there are over twenty-five African bishops, Portugal's African clergy are almost confined to a handful of plain priests.

Largely owing to the passive collaboration of the diplomatic services, the cause of Western democracy has, as we have seen, been another of the victims of Dr. Salazar. Discouraged by the post-war situation, in which Britain, the United States and Brazil collaborated with the Portuguese dictator, or dismissed Portugal as small and unimportant, Portuguese democrats began to look to the West with justified resentment. The change of heart in the United States which, after consistently voting with the Estado Novo at the United Nations, later became a leading patron of Portuguese African emancipation without a corresponding change of policy towards such opposition efforts as those of General Delgado and Henrique Galvao (who have both been denied entry to the United States) has been as hard for Portuguese democrats to accept as it has been for the African leaders themselves to understand.

Were it not for the political importance Portugal derives from its position as ruler of some major territories involved in the wider international issue of African emancipation, the situation of the Portuguese people would continue to go unnoticed in the world. The obscurantism of the country has perhaps been the greatest single contribution to this state of affairs. But the inevitable disintegration of the Portuguese Empire, now so much in the news, will simultaneously focus attention on this centuries-old domestic drama—and not before time, for its cost has been incalculable in terms of human suffering and of the wastage, through illiteracy and repression, of the vitality and intelligence of a small people that once made a significant contribution to human progress.

In the process of imperial disintegration the fate of the Portuguese peasant has been linked with that of the peoples of Africa. Both have consistently been handled like a flock of witless sheep and the world must realize that Portuguese-African conflicts are only anti-Portuguese by coincidence. There exists a tacit affinity between the opponents of Dr. Salazar, whether they are Portuguese or African, and the two threads of democratic self-assertion are intertwined. Dr. Gaintado from Goa, Dr. Agostinho Neto from Angola, Dr. Eduardo Mondlane from Mozambique have been the targets of Portuguese Police as much as any of the exponents of Metropolitan opposition. Currently, what Dr. Salazar most dreads is that Portuguese democrats abroad should join the Front for the National Liberation of Portuguese Colonies and in the process just add "and Portugal" to their style. The fall of Dr. Salazar would hasten the emancipation of Portuguese African territories and, reciprocally, the emancipation of these territories would hasten the fall of Dr. Salazar. Unless the policy of the United States and Britain becomes as consistently liberal as that of Brazil under President Quadros, it will continue to be viewed as a matter of political expediency, and it will not be surprising if Dr. Salazar's "subjects", whether in Africa or Portugal, keep on listening to Communist propaganda, which is, after all, the only forbidden fruit currently within reach of their hunger for freedom.

The Portuguese in Angola (200,000) and Mozambique (90,000)

present a further problem largely of Dr. Salazar's making. The liberal conscience cannot easily dismiss it just because the communities are small in number. While the educated settlers are hardly aware of the secretive activities of the Portuguese administration or the dealings of the Metropolitan Portuguese traders who come and go, the European population in Angola also includes over 25 per cent illiterates who earn a mere £15 to £30 a month and are accustomed to being treated as chattels themselves. The slaughter of these people becomes a moral problem in itself. They react legitimately, as men, to the butchering of their women and children, since they, for their part, do not go around raping and mutilating the children of Africans.

The situation of the Portuguese in Africa is disturbing in all its aspects. No one knows what the nature and extent of the Angolan phenomenon really is. It is clearly aimed, as we have seen, at the introduction of alarming forms of racial hatred. It may be a movement timed to precede a change in the Portuguese Government in order to attract, while it opposes the Fascist Estado Novo, sympathy that might not be forthcoming for any similar resistance to a democratic Portuguese government, genuinely prepared to compromise. It may be a regional extension of the Congo crisis. Other possible implications will only be revealed by the duration of guerrilla warfare. If it takes on an Algerian character, then it is part of a Pan-African, anti-European movement, which could be followed by a major assault on the neighbouring British territories and South Africa. If it is an indirect Communist threat to the vulnerable area of Western influence formed by white-dominated Southern Africa, then the Portuguese, unless they are supported by the West, will have no option but to leave Africa.

Dr. Salazar is obstructing the clarification of these pressing problems and surely nobody is more interested in this clarification than the Portuguese settlers in Africa.

In the face of a situation in which the Government fiercely claims to be in a defensive position, even liberal Portuguese find it hard to make a stand against retaliation, especially since the publicity given to African atrocities is aimed at shaking everybody's conscience. In a world where Soviet Russia mercilessly crushed the Hungarian uprisings, the Americans apparently conspire and finance the overthrow of the Guatemalan and Cuban governments, the British handle roughly the situations in Kenya, Suez and Cyprus, and the French behave similarly in Madagascar and Algeria, few nations are fit to criticize the Portuguese Government for the defence of their people. It is the ruthlessness of their campaign that shocks all decent opinion. The world should now be considering the predicament of the Portuguese democrats themselves and the international capitals to which the protagonists are answerable should be using their influence to achieve a truce. They should be making it understood that diplomatic pressure is preferable to bloodshed.

The only hope lies in a change of government in Portugal, which would open the way for a revision of Portuguese overseas problems in a Pan-Portuguese Conference, at which African leaders, as is their right, would participate. Without a solution of this kind Mozambique and Angola will rush on to apartheid, and repression will only continue to delay the right and inevitable process of emancipation.

Revolution is not Revenge

The new generation accepts the fact that the world is not to blame for the poverty and backwardness of the Portuguese people. These things are obviously the consequence not only of the country's size and lack of resources, but of the nature of Portuguese rule and the stratification of Portuguese society. Great Britain, in proportion to her Commonwealth, is neither so much bigger nor so much richer in natural resources. The slow but steady democratic evolution of British society has been the essential factor determining her progress at home and throughout most of the world. The world is not to blame if the Portuguese have allowed themselves to be so governed that, by the twentieth century, they are surpassed in every direction—that any of the so-called threats hanging over the Empire, be they white autonomy, multi-racial or non-racial independence, economic internationalism or even covetous neo-imperialisms prove to be more dynamic than the traditions of Portuguese rule. Since there is an international retraction of capital investment in unstable Southern Africa, and since such capital is essential to the increased rate of development of Africa's resources, if Portugal continues her present policies she will be left alone, and the scarcity of new capital will only increase the contrast between the development of her territories and that of neighbouring states.

Apart from the problems of the major provinces of Angola and Mozambique, a realistic approach is needed to the forgotten issue of the minor territories under Portuguese rule. Their respective populations can ill afford to be kept on simply as historical relics.

Portuguese Guinea, an enclave extending landward into West Africa, is obviously striving for international association. The social development of 600,000 Portuguese Guineans would naturally be speeded up if they were integrated in the political and economic development of this area. The relatively not-so-distant Cape Verde archipelago, the administration of which was amalgamated with that of Portuguese Guinea up to the later part of the nineteenth century, would clearly benefit from association with the economic development of the mainland. The 150,000 Cape Verde Creoles have every reason to feel lonely and abandoned if their ruling motherland happens to be thousands of miles away. The Sao Thomé and Principe islanders have a right to choose their own future, and, since their islands are extremely fertile, they would be likely to look after themselves better if self-assertion could be attained. The freedom of Goa is a matter of decency and logic, and this is what the intelligent and knowing Goans surely expect from the oppressed anti-Salazar Portuguese when they come to power—after all, Portuguese, Goans and even African opposition leaders have often been comrades in jail. Timor is situated fifteen thousand miles away from Portugal, between Australia and South East Asia. The Portuguese themselves know very little of what happens there, except that it is half of an island of the same name, and that now and again some indigenous people are arrested and deported by the local Portuguese authorities for political reasons—which is not surprising if they start thinking about their situation.

Relieved of the burden of administering this vast and dispersed Empire, the new generation of Portuguese would try and maintain whatever cultural or economic connections could be saved—and they are more likely to be saved by the adoption of a progressive policy than by a policy of repression. A breathing space in which to review the problems of the dislocation of the economy is as necessary to Portugal as it is to the various components of the Empire themselves. Then we should have to turn to this political entity that is Portugal and make of it a country—for only a land where the people have democratic self-assertion can be so defined. Socialism will have to be adopted by means of adequate agrarian and fiscal reforms, which the Portuguese ruling class has been able to postpone by diverting its energies and attentions to the Empire and finding in colonial exploitation the grounds on which to make the present structure work without acute forms of famine.

Looking at the Western democracies, it seems that the adoption of socialism follows the patterns of wealth. Its adoption in the United States goes under other names, and in countries that are not so wealthy, such as Great Britain, Sweden, Norway and Denmark, socialist systems are more strongly and openly applied.

The rising generation of democrats believe that these ambitions are possible of achievement in Portugal because the Portuguese, once granted freedom of the Press and the democratic institutions that have so long been denied to them, will have to face the fact that, without a radical change in the structure of their society, new governments will always be new dictatorships more or less in disguise.

With the Empire gone there will be little need for the Army, and its reduction will be justified on economic grounds alone, since, figuratively speaking, the Portuguese are at present being given an expensive machine-gun to guard a piece of maize bread and a handful of sardines. We need to carry the "civilizing mission" amongst ourselves, for forty per cent of our people are still illiterate and live at subsistence level. We must return once and for all to our Iberian condition. Whatever cultural and linguistic dissimilarities there are between Portuguese and Spaniards are not the cause but the effect of political division, and a policy of economic and political association with a free Spain seems to be the logical trend of Iberian politics and is also consistent with the increasing tendency towards European integration. We hope that the world will help us to achieve self-assertion and that the ironies of history will not lead to the emancipation of the African subjects before that of their so-called rulers. We are no longer prepared to adore the ancestors as a patriotic duty while proving to be unworthy of them. The new patriotism will be different: it will not demand the concealment of our people's backwardness and poverty so that the privileged can enjoy a standard of living out of proportion to the wealth of their country. The new patriotism will be a striving for progress and democracy. When the Empire goes, since this is the last of Empires, liberals throughout the world, who, thank God, are in an overwhelming majority, will surely help us in our economic burdens by seizing upon a bottle of Port wine and drinking to freedom. The only lesson from Portuguese history that will be acceptable in this generation will be the logical advice of a Portuguese statesman in another time of national crisis: "Bury the dead and care for the living."

APPENDICES

FACTS ABOUT THE PORTUGUESE EMPIRE

THE OVERSEAS TERRITORIES of Portugal ceased to have the
status of colonies and were renamed Provinces on 11th June, 1951.
The following is the basic information relating to them:

Angola. Area; 481,352 square miles, including the enclave of
Cabinda. Population estimates (mid-1961): Africans 4,500,000,
Europeans 200,000, half-castes 40,000. Exports: coffee, diamonds,
sugar, cotton, palm oil, palm kernels, beans. Imports: capital goods
and consumer manufactures.

Mozambique. Area: 297,654 square miles. Population (mid-1961
estimates): Africans 6,200,000, Europeans 90,000, half-castes 20,000,
Asians (including Goans) 12,000. Exports: cotton, sugar, sisal, cashew
nuts, vegetable oils, copra. Imports: capital goods, consumer manufactures.

(The comparison between the economic development of these two
territories with South Africa and Southern Rhodesia, where development is essentially based on mineral wealth, is hardly valid. As compared
with other territories on a similar pattern—such as Kenya, Tanganyika, Nyasaland—Mozambique and Angola show well. Some of
the towns of Angola and Mozambique are amongst the most modern
and well-planned of the whole sub-continent, though, as in Portugal,
there is poverty behind the façade.)

Portuguese Guinea. Area: 13,944 square miles consisting of a low
lying coastal area and many islands and islets off shore, including
the Bissagos Archipelago. Population: Africans 600,000, Cape Verde
Creoles 5,000, Europeans 2,600. Exports: groundnuts, palm oil, wax,
rice and timber. Imports: capital goods, consumer manufactures.

Cape Verde. Area: 1,557 square miles. An archipelago consisting
of 14 islands, the major of them being Santo Tiago (383 square miles),
Santo Antao (301 square miles), Fogo (184 square miles), Santo Nicolau

(132 square miles), San Vincente (88 square miles). Population: Creoles 180,000, Europeans 3,200. Exports: coffee, physic-nuts, millet, sugar, spirits. Imports: capital goods, consumer manufactures and coal. The capital is Cidade da Praia. Mindello is an important re-fuelling port for ships of the European–South American lines.

Sao Thomé. Area: 400 square miles. With the island of Principe and the small territory of Sarame, around the fortress of S. Baptista de Ajuda on the coast of Dahomey, it forms the Portuguese Province of S. Thomé and Principe. Population: Africans 70,000, Europeans 1,500. Exports: coffee, cocoa, tropical fruits. Imports: capital goods and consumer manufactures.

Portuguese India. Area: 1,542 square miles (Goa 1,309 square miles, Damao 219 square miles, Diu 14 square miles). Population: Goa 600,000, Damao 80,000, Diu 30,000. Europeans 1,000. Exports: coconuts, cashew nuts, betel, mangoes and dried fish. Imports: capital goods, consumer products and foodstuffs (rice, vegetables, meat, etc.).

Macau (China, near Hong Kong). Area: 5 square miles. Population: Chinese 250,000 (including refugees from Red China), Europeans 2,500. Economics: transit trade.

Timor. Area: 7,329 square miles. Population: Indonesians 500,000, Europeans 700. Exports: coffee and copra.

EXTRACTS FROM THE REPORT WRITTEN BY HENRIQUE GALVAO, JANUARY 1947, ON CONDITIONS IN PORTUGUESE AFRICA

Figures are mute, static. They do not shout, they do not tell of pain. One needs to go and see for one's self, and one needs to encourage those who want to see, instead of condemning them as "inconvenient" to places of exile. One needs to study the phenomena *in loco* across some thousands of miles normally visited by nobody; to gain the confidence of the natives and to listen to them; to hear from administrative officers, who are afraid to report truthfully, the things that only on special occasions they dare to say; to listen to missionaries expressing views in friendly conversation that they do not write in their records . . .

The following are some of the current facts and implications of the problem of labour resulting from the action of employers . . . who dodge inspection, give bribes or take advantage of the passive attitudes of the authorities responsible for the protection of the natives:

(1) Resistance in all possible ways to a policy of paying wages that are economically or socially just.

(2) Bad treatment of workers—corporal punishment and physical violence are still the current practice in Mozambique; the obligations of employers pertaining to clothing, food and health are dodged in a great number of cases. The idea that the native is simply a beast of burden still prevails. Indifference to the physical and moral welfare of the labourers . . . is evident. A division of employers according to the treatment they mete out to their labourers would give a terrific percentage of bad employers.

(3) Wastage of labour. Labour is used as if it were plentiful. Everything is done by the arm-power of the native, from the pushing of trucks to the draining of marshes.

(4) The poor quality and moral character of those entrusted with the recruiting of native labour.

(5) The displacement of labourers from one area to another without regard to climatic differences—especially the hardships to which those coming from the interior to the coastal areas are subjected.

(6) Extortions practised on the natives by merchants.

(7) Indifferent housing conditions.

(8) The vestiges of the exterminating spirit rooted in the last century and the beginnings of this century.

This, in a superficial summary, is the prevailing situation in the field of labour problems. The Government is informed of the full details.

Admittedly we have it recorded in official legislation that the problem is a very difficult one. No one denies it. Today it is more difficult than yesterday. Tomorrow will be more difficult than today. The fact is that we have known this for ten years and that in these ten years there has been not a single effective measure to solve the problem. . . .

SUGGESTED READING

Davidson, Basil. *The African Awakening*. Cape (London), 1955.

Duffy, James. *Portuguese Africa*. Harvard Univ. Press (Cambridge Press), 1959.

Harris, Marvin. *Portugal's African Wards*. American Committee on Africa, 1958.

Harris, Marvin. Contributions to *Africa* (London) and *Africa Today* (New York).

Nevinson, Henry Wood. *Modern Slavery in Angola, etc.* Harper (London and New York), 1906.

Sampson, Anthony. *Common Sense about Africa*. Gollancz (London), 1960.

Useful information can also be found in *Goa*, edited in London by The Goa League, London; and in *The Portuguese and Colonial Bulletin*, edited in London by a group of Portuguese democrats.

INDEX